MILITARY AVIATION LIBRARY
# World War II
## British
# Aircraft

# MILITARY AVIATION LIBRARY
## World War II
## British Aircraft

### Bill Gunston

CHARTWELL
BOOKS, INC.

Published by Chartwell Books Inc., New York

© Salamander Books Ltd., 1985

Colour profiles, cutaways and three-view drawings © Pilot Press Ltd.

**ISBN: 0 89009 901 4**

## PICTURE CREDITS

Charles E. Brown: 37 (top), 42 (bottom), 44 (bottom), 54 (bottom).
Hawker Siddeley: 11 (top), 15, 24, 39, 40, 42 (centre), 43 (top).
Hawker Siddeley (Philip Byrtles Collection): 26 (top).
Imperial War Museum: 8, 9, 10, 11 (bottom), 12, 14, 16, 17, 18-19, 20, 21, 22, 25 (top), 26 (bottom), 28, 29, 30, 31, 32, 33, 34, 36, 37 (bottom), 38, 41, 42 (top), 43 (bottom), 44 (top), 45, 46, 47, 48 (top), 50, 54 (top), 55, 58 (top), 59, 60.
J. MacClancy Collection: 51.
J. G. Moore Collection: 23, 49.
Pilot Press Ltd: 35, 48 (bottom).
J. Scutts Collection: 57, 58 (bottom).
US Navy: 61 (top right).
Westland Helicopters Ltd: 61 (top left and bottom).

# Contents

# Airspeed AS.51 Horsa

## Horsa I and II

**Origin:** Airspeed (1934) Ltd (from January 1944 Airspeed Ltd).
**Type:** Assault glider.
**Engine:** None.
**Dimensions:** Span 88ft 0in (26·84m); length 67ft 0in (20·43m); height 19ft 6in (5·9m).
**Weights:** Empty 7,500lb (3402kg); loaded 15,250lb (6917kg).
**Performance:** Typical towing speed 127mph (204km/h); gliding speed 100mph (161km/h).
**History:** Prototype (DG597) flew 12 September 1941; first delivery (DP279) May 1942.
**Users:** Portugal, Turkey, UK (RAF), US (AAF).

**Development:** Germany's success with airborne assault in the Low Countries in May 1940 was so self-evident that the British decided to emulate and, if possible, improve on it. Urgent work went ahead with a number of types of training, troop-carrying and cargo glider and of these by far the most important was the Airspeed AS.51 Horsa, designed to specification X.26/40 as a multirole assault aircraft. It was the biggest glider that could reasonably be towed by available twin-engined tugs. At first training proceeded with Whitley V tugs, with Horsas camouflaged above and painted below with the diagonal black/yellow stripes first seen on target-towing aircraft. By 1943, the usual tug was the Albemarle and the operational gliders had black sides and undersurfaces. Very large orders were placed, not only with Airspeed at Christchurch but also with the Harris Lebus furniture firm, Austin Motor Co and Tata Industries of India. The Indian contract was cancelled but in Britain 3,655 Horsas were built and most saw action. In flight the Horsa creaked loudly and smelled of the wood from which it was made. The Mk I had towing brackets on the wings, necessitating a bifurcated

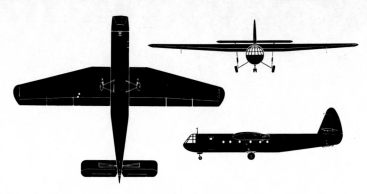

Above: Horsa I with landing gear in position.

rope. The Mk II had a single socket under the nose for a rope which by 1944 was often springy nylon. The rear fuselage could be jettisoned, and there was a large door on the left side; the whole nose of the Mk II could also swing open. With its huge flaps lowered by compressed air and air brakes above and below the wings, the Horsa could almost stand on its nose and swoop quietly into small fields, carrying up to 25 troops. Halifaxes towed two on a special mission to Norway in November 1942. The same type of tug was used in the invasion of Sicily. Hundreds of Horsas took nearly a quarter of the air-supplied loads in the Normandy invasion and, in March 1945, 440 carried the 6th Airborne Division across the Rhine. Many also served with the US Army.

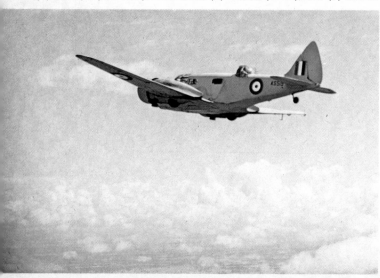

**Left: DP726 was one of a batch of 100 Horsa I gliders built by the Austin Motor Company.** It is depicted in normal training configuration, but on an operational mission was designed to jettison the entire main landing gears and alight on a large sprung ash skid under the centre fuselage.

# Airspeed Oxford

## AS.10 (Oxford I, II) and AS.46 (III, V)

**Origin:** Airspeed (1934) Ltd, Portsmouth; also made at Christchurch and by de Havilland, Percival and Standard Motors.
**Type:** Advanced trainer; see text.
**Engines:** (I) two 355hp Armstrong Siddeley Cheetah IX seven-cylinder radial; (II) 375hp Cheetah X; (III) 425hp Cheetah XV; (IV) 300hp DH Gipsy Queen IV in-line; (V) 450hp Pratt & Whitney R-985-AN6 Wasp Junior nine-cylinder radial.
**Dimensions:** Span 53ft 4in (16·25m); length 34ft 6in (10·52m); height 11ft 1in (3·38m).
**Weights:** Empty, equipped (II) 5,380lb (2440kg), (V) 5,670lb (2575kg); maximum (II) 7,600lb (3450kg), (V) 8,000lb (3629kg).
**Performance** (without turret): Maximum speed (I, II) 188mph (301km/h), (V) 202mph (325km/h); initial climb (II) 1,480ft (450m)/min, (V) 2,000ft

Above: Oxford II nav/radio trainer (but retaining bomb bay).

(610m)/min; service ceiling (typical) 20,000ft (6100m); range (typical) 550 miles (885km).
**Armament:** See text.
**History:** First flight 19 June 1937; service delivery November 1937; final delivery 14 July 1945.
**Users** (WWII): Australia, Canada, Egypt, France, New Zealand, Portugal, S Rhodesia, Turkey, UK (RAF, RN), USA (AAF).

**Development:** The "Ox-box" has never been one of the famed aircraft of history, yet its contribution to World War II was immense. Throughout the Commonwealth it was the chief vehicle in which were trained the scores of thousands of aircrew for the RAF and many other Allied air forces, and the number built (8,751) made it one of the major production programmes of all time. Built of wood, it was a trim machine which demanded precision of its pilots, and would never tolerate a sloppy landing. Early examples had an AW dorsal turret, and in 1940 a few carried additional guns. Nearly all had provision for bombing training, and other roles included training in navigation, photography, radio and twin-engine pilot conversion. Many hundreds served in communications, ambulance, AA co-operation and radio/radar calibration. The IV was an engine test-bed. The III and V had constant-speed propellers and higher performance.

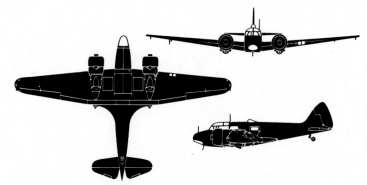

**Left: AS515 was an Oxford I with turret. It is shown in use at an air-gunnery school in Canada.**

# Armstrong Whitworth A.W.38 Whitley

## Whitley I to VIII (data for V)

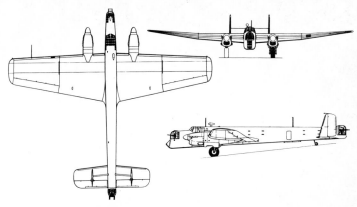

**Origin:** Sir W. G. Armstrong Whitworth Aircraft.
**Type:** Five-seat heavy bomber.
**Engines:** Two 1,145hp Rolls-Royce Merlin X vee-12 liquid-cooled.
**Dimensions:** Span 84ft 0in (25·6m); length 70ft 6in (21·5m); height 15ft 0in (4·57m).
**Weights:** Empty 19,330lb (8768kg); maximum 33,500lb (15,196kg).
**Performance:** Maximum speed 222mph (357km/h); cruising speed, about 185mph (297km/h); initial climb 800ft (244m)/min; service ceiling from 17,600–21,000ft (5400–6400m); range with maximum bomb load 470 miles (756km); range with 3,000lb (1361kg) bombs 1,650 miles (2650km).
**Armament:** One 0·303 in Vickers K in nose turret; four 0·303 in Brownings in tail turret; up to 7,000lb (3175kg) bombs in cells in fuselage and inner wings.

**Above: Typical Whitley V with landing gear extended.**

**Left: This Whitley V served in the early part of the war with 102 Sqn. It took part in many leaflet raids, minelaying sorties and early missions to bomb targets in Germany and northern Italy.**

**History:** First flight (prototype) 17 March 1936; first delivery (Mk I) January 1937; first flight (Mk V) December 1938; first delivery (Mk V) August 1939; production termination June 1943.
**User:** UK (RAF, BOAC).

**Development:** Designed to Specification B.3/34, this heavy bomber was at least an all-metal monoplane with retractable landing gear, but the original Mk I was still primitive. Its thick wing, which in the first batch had no dihedral, was set at a marked positive incidence, so that at normal cruising speeds the long slab-sided Whitley flew in a characteristic nose-down attitude. Powered by 795hp Armstrong Siddeley Tiger IX radials, the Mk I was soon replaced by the Mk II, and then by the III with the 920hp Tiger VIII. In 1938 production switched to the greatly improved Mk IV, with Merlin engines and a power-driven rear turret mounting four machine guns. The Mk IVA had a more powerful Merlin, and this was retained in the

Mk V which was 15in longer and had straight-edged fins. AWA made 1,466 Whitley Vs, the last in June 1943, and also delivered 146 longer-range GR.VIII patrol aircraft with ASV radar for Coastal Command. Whitleys bore the brunt of long leaflet raids, starting on the first night of the war. On 19 March 1940 Whitleys dropped the first bombs to fall on Germany since 1918, and during the next two years these tough and capable aircraft made missions as far as Turin and Pilsen, often in terrible conditions, highlighting deficiencies in navigation and equipment the hard way. Coastal's first U-boat kill was U-206, sunk by a Whitley VII in November 1941. From 1942 the Whitley served mainly as a trainer for paratroops, as a glider tug and with 100 Group as a carrier of experimental or special-purpose radars and countermeasures. Total production was 1,737.

**Below: Ground and aircrew investigate a last minute engine snag before the day air test that always preceded a mission.**

# Armstrong Whitworth A.W.41 Albemarle

## Albemarle I to VI

**Origin:** "A. W. Hawksley".
**Type:** Four-crew special transport and glider tug.
**Engines:** Two 1,590hp Bristol Hercules XI 14-cylinder sleeve-valve radials.
**Dimensions:** Span 77ft 0in (23·47m); length 59ft 11in (18·25m); height 15ft 7in (4·75m).
**Weights:** Empty (GT.VI) 22,600lb (10,260kg); maximum 36,500lb (16,570kg).
**Performance:** Maximum speed 265mph (426km/h); initial climb 980ft (299m)/min; service ceiling 18,000ft (5490m); typical range 1,350 miles (2160km).
**Armament:** None except in Mk I/1 (Boulton Paul dorsal turret with four 0·303in Brownings and powered ventral turret with two 0·303in Brownings) and ST.I (manual dorsal installation with various guns).
**History:** First flight 20 March 1940; (production aircraft) December 1941; final delivery December 1944.
**User:** Soviet Union, UK (RAF).

**Development:** After Bristol had proposed the Type 155 bomber with a nosewheel landing gear (which at that time had not been used in Britain except experimentally) the Air Ministry issued Specification B.18/38 which was notable for its insistence on minimal use of light alloys, which were likely to be in short supply in event of war. Instead the design was to be made mainly of steel and wood, even though this would increase weight. Bristol dropped the 155, and the specification was met by the AW.41, first flown on 20 March 1940. Production was entirely subcontracted to firms outside the aircraft industry, and parts were brought to a plant at Gloucester for which Hawker Siddeley formed a company called A. W. Hawksley Ltd. Thus, not only did the Albemarle conserve strategic materials (with very small penalty, as it turned out) but it had no parent factory or design organization. Delivery began in October 1941, but only 32 were completed as bombers and these were converted as transports. Altogether 600 were delivered by the end of 1944, in many versions grouped into two main families: ST, or Special Transport, used all over Europe and North Africa; and GT, Glider Tug, used in Sicily, Normandy and at Arnhem. Glider towing needed high power at low airspeeds, and the Hercules overheated and poured oil smoke, but the Albemarle was otherwise pleasant to fly.

Above: An Albemarle, probably an ST.II, on takeoff with Horsa I at the Heavy Glider Conversion Unit, Brize Norton.

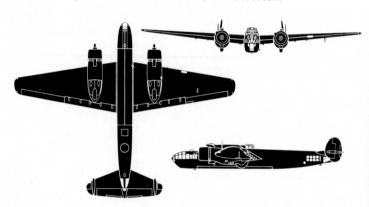

Above: The original Albemarle I Series I before conversion.

# Avro 652M Anson

## 652A Anson I and later marks to T.22, USAAF AT-20

**Origin:** A. V. Roe Ltd, Chadderton, Bracebridge Heath, Newton Heath and Yeadon; in Canada by Federal Aircraft.
**Type:** Originally reconnaissance bomber, later crew trainer and multirole.
**Engines:** (I, X) two 355hp Armstrong Siddeley IX seven-cylinder radial; (II, III) 330hp Jacobs L-6MB (R-915) of same layout; (IV) 450hp Wright R-975-E3 Whirlwind; (V, VI) 450hp Pratt & Whitney R-985-AN14B Wasp Junior; (XI, XII) 420hp Cheetah XIX or XV.
**Dimensions:** Span 56ft 6in (17·22m); length (nearly all) 42ft 3in (12·88 m); height 13ft 1in (3·99m).
**Weights:** Empty, equipped (I) 5,375lb (2438kg), (V) 6,693lb (3036kg), (XII) 6,510lb (2953kg); maximum (I) 8,000lb (3629kg), (V) 9,460lb (4291kg), (XII) 9,900lb (4491kg).
**Performance** (no turret): Maximum speed (I) 188mph (303km/h), (V) 190mph (306km/h), (XII) 175mph (282km/h); typical cruise 150mph (241km/h); typical range 700 miles (1127km).
**Armament:** See text.
**History:** First flight 24 March 1935; service delivery 6 March 1936; final delivery May 1952.

**Users** (WW2): Australia, Canada, Egypt, France, Greece, Iran, Ireland, Netherlands, UK (RAF, RN, ATA, BOAC), US (AAF).

**Development:** The abiding memory of "Faithful Annie" is of the most docile and reliable machine in the whole war. Yet when it was first delivered to 48 Sqn RAF Coastal Command it was very much a "hot ship". It was a monoplane, and it had retractable landing gear (laboriously cranked up and down by hand), and despite a large dorsal turret it was almost the fastest thing in the service. One attacked a U-boat only two days after the start of the war, and in June 1940 a close vic of three survived attacks by nine Bf 109Es, shooting down at least two of the German fighters despite having only a single drum-fed Lewis in each turret. Later many Mk I trainers had twin belt-fed Brownings in a Bristol turret, and virtually all Mk Is carried at least provision for bombing training. Altogether 6,704 Mk I were built, and thousands were used for general communications or converted into Mk X transports with smooth engine cowls and strong freight floors. DH Canada fitted some with American engines to produce the III and IV. Federal built 2,882 Ansons from 1941, most being Mk II (USAAF AT-20) but later batches being the V and VI with fuselages of Vidal moulded ply instead of steel tube and fabric. The XI and XII at last introduced hydraulic landing gear (on the Canadian machines from the start) and a much roomier fuselage, as well as constant-speed propellers and many other changes. These evolved into the modern stressed-skin C.19 and T.20, 21 and 22 for the post-war RAF. Total production was 11,020.

Below: Though the vast majority of Ansons were trainers, utility transports and hacks, this original Mk I is seen in 1942 still with 217 Sqn Coastal Command after six years.

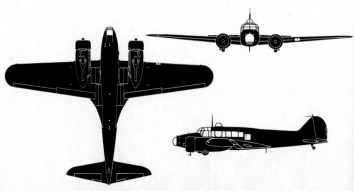

Above: Anson X with astro-dome (often absent).

# Avro 679 Manchester

## 679 Manchester I and IA

**Origin:** A. V. Roe Ltd, Chadderton.
**Type:** Heavy bomber.
**Engines:** Two Rolls-Royce Vulture I 24-cylinder X-form, rated at 1,760hp but in fact derated to 1,480–1,500hp.
**Dimensions:** Span 90ft 1in (27·46m); length 70ft 0in (21·34m); height 19ft 6in (5·94m).
**Weights:** Empty 31,200lb (14,152kg); maximum 56,000lb but in fact never authorised above 50,000lb (22,680kg).
**Performance:** Maximum speed (typical) 250mph (402km/h); service ceiling (42,000lb) 19,500ft (5852m); range with maximum bomb load 1,200 miles (1930km).
**Armament:** Eight 0·303in Browning in power turrets in nose (2), mid-upper (2) and tail (4); internal fuselage bay accommodating bomb load up to 10,350lb (4695kg).
**History:** First flight 25 July 1939; service delivery November 1940; withdrawal from production November 1941.
**User:** UK (RAF).

**Development:** Rolls-Royce's decision in 1935 to produce a very powerful engine by fitting two sets of Peregrine cylinder-blocks to one crankcase (the lower pair being inverted, to give an X arrangement) prompted the Air Ministry to issue specification P.13/36 for a twin-engined heavy bomber of unprecedented capability. Handley Page changed to four Merlins (see Halifax) but Avro produced the Manchester with the Vulture engine. In most respects it was the best of all the new heavy bombers, but the engine was grossly down on power, and had to be derated further because of extreme unreliability. Originally the Manchester had two fins; in the production Mk I a fixed central fin was added, and the bulk of the 209 delivered had two larger fins (no central fin) and were designated IA. So hopeless was the engine situation that the plans to build Manchesters at Armstrong Whitworth and Fairey were cancelled, and Metropolitan-Vickers stopped at No 32. Avro went on until the vastly superior Lancaster could take over, the first batches of Lancasters having Manchester fuselages with a row of small windows along each side.

Above: L7516, "S-Sugar" of 207 Sqn, the first unit to receive the Manchester in November 1940. This aircraft was a Mk IA.

Below: Mk IA with two enlarged fins on increased-span tailplane.

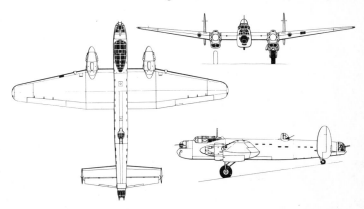

# Avro 683 Lancaster

## 683 Lancaster I to MR.7 (data for I)

**Origin:** A. V. Roe Ltd; also Armstrong Whitworth, Austin Motors, Metropolitan-Vickers and Vickers-Armstrongs, UK, and Victory Aircraft, Canada.
**Type:** Seven-seat heavy bomber.
**Engines:** Four 1,460hp Rolls-Royce or Packard Merlin 20 or 22 (Mk II only: four 1,650hp Bristol Hercules VI, 14 cylinder two-row, sleeve-valve radials).
**Dimensions:** Span 102ft 0in (31·1m); length 69ft 4in (21·1m); height 19ft 7in (5·97m).
**Weights:** Empty 36,900lb (16,705kg); loaded 68,000lb (30,800kg); overload with 22,000lb bomb 70,000lb (31,750kg).

**Performance:** Maximum speed 287mph (462km/h) at 11,500ft (3500m); cruising speed 210mph (338km/h); climb at maximum weight to 20,000ft (6095m) 41 minutes; service ceiling 24,500ft (7467m); range with 14,000lb (6350kg) bombs 1,660 miles (2675km).
**Armament:** Nose and dorsal turrets (Mk II also ventral) with two 0·303in Brownings (some, including Mk VII, had Martin dorsal turret with two 0·5in), tail turret with four 0·303in Brownings, 33ft 0in (10·06m) bomb bay carrying normal load of 14,000lb (6350kg) or 22,000lb (9979kg) bomb with modification.
**History:** First flight 9 January 1941; service delivery (for test and training) September 1941; last delivery from new 2 February 1946.

▶

Below: An inspiring sight to anyone who remembers those great days—the final assembly line at A. V. Roe's Woodford plant in 1943 (Mk Is with serials in the batch JA672-JB748).

► **Users:** Australia, Canada, New Zealand, Poland, UK (RAF, BOAC).

**Development:** Undoubtedly one of the major influences on World War II, and one of the greatest aircraft of history, the "Lanc" came about because of the failure of its predecessor. In September 1936 the Air Staff issued specification P.13/36 for a twin-engined bomber of exceptional size and capability to be powered by two of the very powerful engines then under development: the Rolls-Royce Vulture 24-cylinder X engine was preferred. Handley Page switched to four Merlins with the Halifax, but A. V. Roe adhered to the big-twin formula and the first Type 679 Manchester flew on 25 July 1939. Altogether 209 Manchesters were delivered by November 1941, but the type was plagued by the poor performance and unreliability of its engine. Though it equipped eight Bomber Command squadrons, and parts of two others plus a flight in Coastal Command, the Manchester was withdrawn from service in June 1942 and survivors were scrapped.

Nevertheless the basic Manchester was clearly outstandingly good, and in 1940 the decision was taken to build a longer-span version with four Merlin engines. The first Lancaster (BT 308) flew as the Manchester III at the beginning of 1941. So outstanding was its performance that it went into immediate large-scale production, and Manchesters already on the line from L7527 onwards were completed as Lancasters (distinguished from later aircraft by their row of rectangular windows in the rear fuselage). Deliveries began in early 1942 to 44 Sqn at Waddington, and on 17 April 1942 a mixed force of 44 and 97 Sqns made a rather foolhardy daylight raid against the MAN plant at Augsburg, whereupon the new bomber's existence was revealed.

**Above: Late-war Lancs letting go thousand-pounders over a cloud-covered target in daylight, common from spring 1944.**

**Below: Cutaway drawing of a Lancaster III, similar to a Mk I except for Packard nameplates and US accessories on the engines. Usual night load was a 4,000-pounder plus incendiaries.**

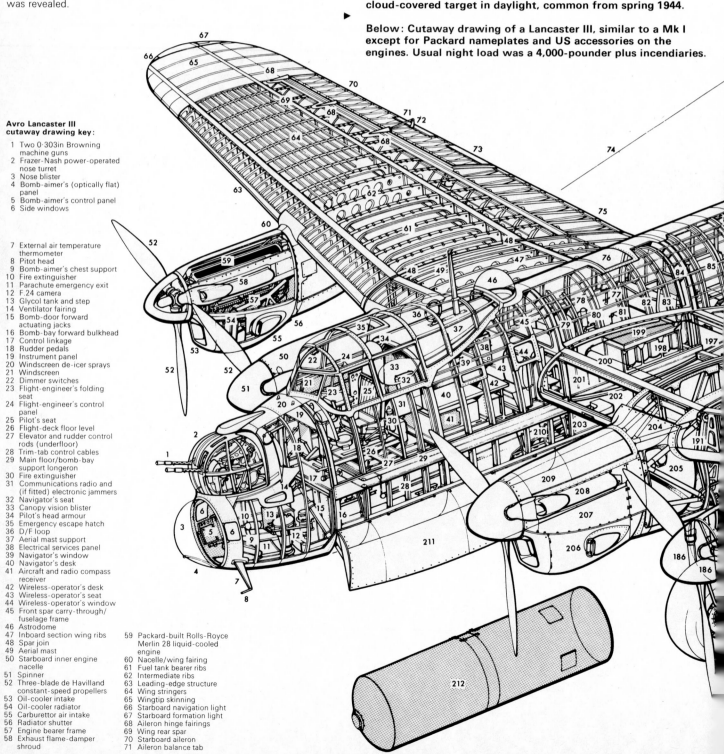

**Avro Lancaster III cutaway drawing key:**

1. Two 0·303in Browning machine guns
2. Frazer-Nash power-operated nose turret
3. Nose blister
4. Bomb-aimer's (optically flat) panel
5. Bomb-aimer's control panel
6. Side windows
7. External air temperature thermometer
8. Pitot head
9. Bomb-aimer's chest support
10. Fire extinguisher
11. Parachute emergency exit
12. F.24 camera
13. Glycol tank and step
14. Ventilator fairing
15. Bomb-door forward actuating jacks
16. Bomb-bay forward bulkhead
17. Control linkage
18. Rudder pedals
19. Instrument panel
20. Windscreen de-icer sprays
21. Windscreen
22. Dimmer switches
23. Flight-engineer's folding seat
24. Flight-engineer's control panel
25. Pilot's seat
26. Flight-deck floor level
27. Elevator and rudder control rods (underfloor)
28. Trim-tab control cables
29. Main floor/bomb-bay support longeron
30. Fire extinguisher
31. Communications radio and (if fitted) electronic jammers
32. Navigator's seat
33. Canopy vision blister
34. Pilot's head armour
35. Emergency escape hatch
36. D/F loop
37. Aerial mast support
38. Electrical services panel
39. Navigator's window
40. Navigator's desk
41. Aircraft and radio compass receiver
42. Wireless-operator's desk
43. Wireless-operator's seat
44. Wireless-operator's window
45. Front spar carry-through/ fuselage frame
46. Astrodome
47. Inboard section wing ribs
48. Spar join
49. Aerial mast
50. Starboard inner engine nacelle
51. Spinner
52. Three-blade de Havilland constant-speed propellers
53. Oil-cooler intake
54. Oil-cooler radiator
55. Carburettor air intake
56. Radiator shutter
57. Engine bearer frame
58. Exhaust flame-damper shroud
59. Packard-built Rolls-Royce Merlin 28 liquid-cooled engine
60. Nacelle/wing fairing
61. Fuel tank bearer ribs
62. Intermediate ribs
63. Leading-edge structure
64. Wing stringers
65. Wingtip skinning
66. Starboard navigation light
67. Starboard formation light
68. Aileron hinge fairings
69. Wing rear spar
70. Starboard aileron
71. Aileron balance tab

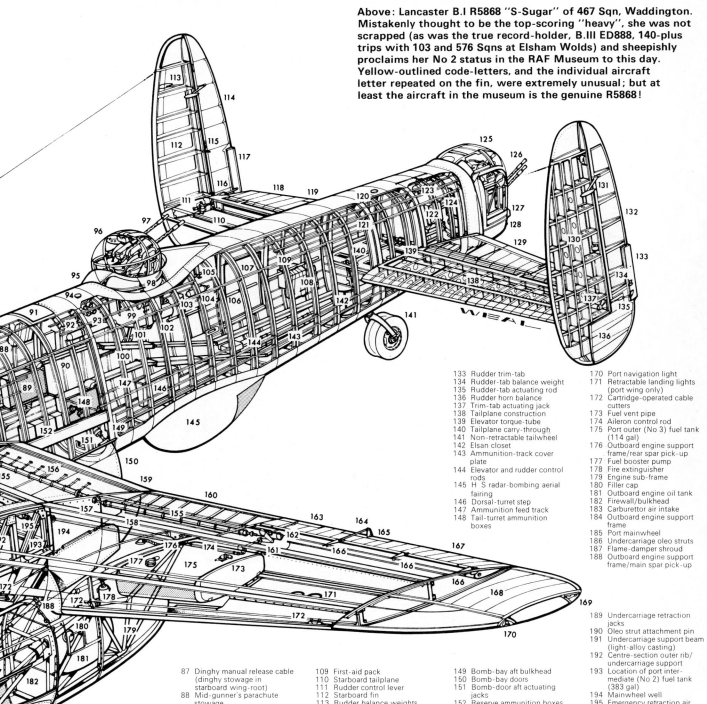

**Above: Lancaster B.I R5868 "S-Sugar" of 467 Sqn, Waddington. Mistakenly thought to be the top-scoring "heavy", she was not scrapped (as was the true record-holder, B.III ED888, 140-plus trips with 103 and 576 Sqns at Elsham Wolds) and sheepishly proclaims her No 2 status in the RAF Museum to this day. Yellow-outlined code-letters, and the individual aircraft letter repeated on the fin, were extremely unusual; but at least the aircraft in the museum is the genuine R5868!**

133 Rudder trim-tab
134 Rudder-tab balance weight
135 Rudder-tab actuating rod
136 Rudder horn balance
137 Trim-tab actuating jack
138 Tailplane construction
139 Elevator torque-tube
140 Tailplane carry-through
141 Non-retractable tailwheel
142 Elsan closet
143 Ammunition-track cover plate
144 Elevator and rudder control rods
145 H S radar-bombing aerial fairing
146 Dorsal-turret step
147 Ammunition feed track
148 Tail-turret ammunition boxes

170 Port navigation light
171 Retractable landing lights (port wing only)
172 Cartridge-operated cable cutters
173 Fuel vent pipe
174 Aileron control rod
175 Port outer (No 3) fuel tank (114 gal)
176 Outboard engine support frame/rear spar pick-up
177 Fuel booster pump
178 Fire extinguisher
179 Engine sub-frame
180 Filler cap
181 Outboard engine oil tank
182 Firewall/bulkhead
183 Carburettor air intake
184 Outboard engine support frame
185 Port mainwheel
186 Undercarriage oleo struts
187 Flame-damper shroud
188 Outboard engine support frame/main spar pick-up

189 Undercarriage retraction jacks
190 Oleo strut attachment pin
191 Undercarriage support beam (light-alloy casting)
192 Centre-section outer rib/ undercarriage support
193 Location of port inter-mediate (No 2) fuel tank (383 gal)
194 Mainwheel well
195 Emergency retraction air valve
196 Retraction cylinder attachment
197 Port inner (No 1) fuel tank (580 gal)
198 Oxygen-bottle stowage
199 Rest bunk
200 Main spar
201 Hinged inboard leading-edge
202 Cabin heater installation
203 Air intake
204 Inboard engine support frame
205 Inboard engine oil tank
206 Carburettor intake anti-ice guard
207 Inboard nacelle
208 Flame-damper shroud
209 Detachable cowling panels
210 Bomb shackles
211 Bomb-bay doors (open)
212 8,000 lb bomb

72 Balance-tab control rod
73 Aileron trim-tab
74 HF aerial
75 Split trailing-edge flap (outboard section)
76 Emergency (ditching) exit
77 Crash axe stowage
78 Fire extinguisher
79 Hydraulic reservoir
80 Signal/flare pistol stowage
81 Parachute stowage box/spar step
82 Rear spar carry-through
83 Bunk backrest
84 Rear spar fuselage frame
85 Emergency packs
86 Roof light

87 Dinghy manual release cable (dinghy stowage in starboard wing-root)
88 Mid-gunner's parachute stowage
89 Tail turret ammunition box
90 Ammunition feed track
91 Emergency (ditching) exit
92 Flame floats stowage
93 Sea markers stowage
94 Roof light
95 Dorsal turret fairing
96 Frazer-Nash power-operated dorsal turret
97 Two 0·303in Browning machine-guns
98 Turret mounting ring
99 Turret mechanism
100 Ammunition track cover plate
101 Turret step bracket
102 Header tank
103 Oxygen cylinder
104 Fire extinguisher
105 DR compass housing
106 Handrail
107 Crew entry door (starboard)
108 Parachute stowage

109 First-aid pack
110 Starboard tailplane
111 Rudder control lever
112 Starboard fin
113 Rudder balance weights
114 Starboard rudder
115 Rudder datum hinge
116 Rudder-tab actuating rod
117 Rudder tab
118 Starboard elevator
119 Elevator balance tab
120 Roof light
121 Tail main frame
122 Parachute stowage
123 Fire extinguisher
124 Tail-turret entry door
125 Frazer-Nash power-operated tail turret
126 Four 0·303in Browning machine guns
127 Cartridge-case ejection chutes
128 Rear navigation light and Monica tail-warning radar
129 Elevator trim-tab
130 Fin construction
131 Rudder balance weights
132 Port rudder frame

149 Bomb-bay aft bulkhead
150 Bomb-bay doors
151 Bomb-door aft actuating jacks
152 Reserve ammunition boxes
153 Main floor support structure
154 Flap-operating hydraulic jack
155 Flap-operating tube
156 Flap toggle links
157 Flap-tube connecting link
158 Rear spar
159 Split trailing-edge flap (inboard)
160 Split trailing-edge flap (outboard)
161 Aileron control lever
162 Aileron trim-tab control linkage
163 Aileron trim tab
164 Aileron balance-tab control rod
165 Aileron balance tab
166 Aileron hinge fairings
167 Port aileron
168 Port wingtip
169 Port formation light

13

From then until the end of World War II Lancasters made 156,000 sorties in Europe and dropped 608,612 long tons of bombs. Total production, including 430 in Canada by Victory Aircraft, was 7,377. Of these 3,425 were Mk I and 3,039 the Mk III with US Packard-built engines. A batch of 300 was built as Mk IIs with the more powerful Bristol Hercules radial, some with bulged bomb bays and a ventral turret. The Mk I (Special) was equipped to carry the 12,000lb (5443kg) light-case bomb and the 12,000lb and 22,000lb (9979kg) Earthquake bombs, the $H_2S$ radar blister under the rear fuselage being removed. The Mk I (FE) was equipped for Far East operations with Tiger Force. The aircraft of 617 (Dambusters) Sqn were equipped to spin and release the Wallis skipping drum bomb. The Mk VI had high-altitude Merlins and four-blade propellers and with turrets removed served 635 Sqn and 100 Grp as a countermeasure and radar spoof carrier. Other marks served as photo-reconnaissance and maritime reconnaissance and air/sea rescue aircraft, the last MR.7 leaving RAF front-line service in February 1954.

Lancasters took part in every major night attack on Germany. They soon showed their superiority by dropping 132 long tons of bombs for each aircraft lost, compared with 56 (later 86) for the Halifax and 41 for the Stirling. They carried a heavier load of bigger bombs than any other aircraft in the European theatre. The 12,000lb AP bomb was used to sink the *Tirpitz*, and the 22,000lb weapon finally shook down the stubborn viaduct at Bielefeld in March 1945. Around Caen, Lancasters were used en masse in the battlefield close-support role, and they finished the war dropping supplies to starving Europeans and ferrying home former prisoners of war.

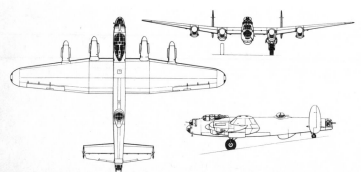

Above: Incendiaries cascade from one of the highly secret B.Is of No 101 Sqn, from Ludford Magna, with Airborne Cigar electronic jamming equipment (note the two tall dorsal masts).

Left: Three-view of a typical Mk I or Mk III Lancaster.

Below: Colour photography was rare in Britain in World War II. This splendid picture was taken from beside the pilot of a Lanc of 50 Sqn at Swinderby (Press visit, 28 August 1942).

# Blackburn Skua and Roc

## Skua II, Roc I

**Origin:** The Blackburn Aircraft Company, Brough; Roc production assigned to Boulton Paul Aircraft, Wolverhampton.
**Type:** (S) two-seat carrier fighter/dive bomber; (R) two-seat carrier fighter.
**Engine:** 905hp Bristol Perseus XII nine-cylinder sleeve-valve radial.
**Dimensions:** Span (S) 46ft 2in (14·07m), (R) 46ft 0in (14·02m); length (S) 35ft 7in (10·85m), (R) 35ft 0in (10·67m); height 12ft 5in (3·79m).
**Weights:** Empty (S) 5,490lb (2490kg), (R) 6,121lb (2776kg); maximum (S) 8,228lb (3732kg), (R) 8,800lb (3992kg).
**Performance:** Maximum speed (S) 225mph (362km/h), (R) 196mph (315km/h); service ceiling 20,200ft (6157m); range (typical) 800 miles (1287km).
**Armament:** (S) four 0·303in Browning fixed in wings, one 0·303in Lewis or Vickers K in rear cockpit, 500lb (227kg) bomb on hinged arms under fuselage, light bombs under wings; (R) four 0·303in Browning in power dorsal turret, light bombs under wings.

**History:** First flight (S) 9 February 1937, (R) 23 December 1938; service delivery (S) November 1938, (R) April 1939.
**User:** UK (RN).

**Development:** The Skua was designed to a 1934 specification, O.27/34, for a naval dive bomber. Two prototypes powered by 840hp Mercury engines looked sleek against the Navy's fabric-covered biplanes, and eventually 190 were built to a later requirement (25/36), to enter service as the Fleet Air Arm's first monoplane and first with v-p propeller or retractable landing gear. During the first year of war the Skuas worked hard, and made many gallant attacks on German capital ships. On 26 September 1939 Skuas of 803 Sqn from *Ark Royal* shot down a Do 18, the first Luftwaffe aircraft destroyed by Britain. But the basic aircraft was underpowered, and by 1941 the Skua was becoming a target tug and trainer. Likewise the 136 turreted Rocs were even less capable of surviving, let alone acting as fighters. The 136 built, to O.30/35, never served on a carrier and were soon withdrawn. A few were seaplanes, with Shark-type floats.

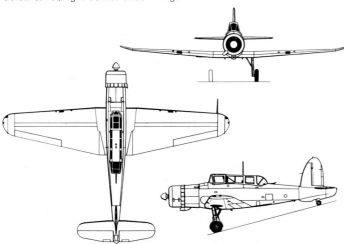

Above: Skua II showing four wing guns and upturned tips.

Right: Pre-war picture of a Skua making a practice bombing dive, with patented Zapp flaps fully depressed to limit speed.

Below: Though pleasant to fly, one wonders how the Roc, a 196mph fighter, could have been considered for combat duty.

# Boulton Paul P.82 Defiant

## Defiant I and II (data for I)

**Origin:** Boulton Paul Aircraft, Wolverhampton.
**Type:** Two-seat fighter.
**Engine:** I, 1,030hp Rolls-Royce Merlin III vee-12 liquid-cooled; II, 1,260hp Merlin 20.
**Dimensions:** Span 39ft 4in (12m); length 35ft 4in (10·75m); height 12ft 2in (3·7m).
**Weights:** Empty 6,000lb (2722kg); loaded 8,350lb (3787kg).
**Performance:** Maximum speed 303mph (488km/h); initial climb 1,900ft (579m)/min; service ceiling 30,500ft (9300m); range, probably about 500 miles (805km).
**Armament:** Hydraulically operated dorsal gun turret with four 0·303in Browning machine guns, each with 600 rounds.
**History:** First flight (prototype) 11 August 1937; (production Mk I) 30 July 1939; first delivery December 1939.
**User:** UK (RAF).

**Development:** By 1933 military staffs were intensely studying the enclosed gun turret, manually worked or power-driven, either to defend a bomber or to arm a fighter. A primitive form was seen on the Hawker Demon in 1936, while in France the *Multiplace de Combat* class of aircraft were huge fighters with turrets all over. The Defiant was a bold attempt to combine the performance of the new monoplanes with a powered enclosed turret carrying four 0·303in Brownings, each with 600 rounds. The gunner, behind the pilot, had a control column moved left/right for rotation, fore/aft for depression and elevation and with a safety/firing button on top. The Defiant itself was a clean and pleasant aircraft, but rather degraded in performance by carrying a crew of two and the heavy turret. No 264 Sqn went into action on 12 May 1940 in desperate fights over the Low Countries. On the 13th six escorted Battle bombers, and only one returned; it seemed the

**Right: Defiant II of 125 Sqn on night operations in 1941-42 but lacking radar. Note fold-down radio masts.**

**Below: Fighter Command's 264 Sqn was the first recipient of the Defiant, and this photograph was taken during the working-up period in early 1940. In fact the concept of the sluggish two-seat fighter was faulty, and production of 1,060 (continued until February 1943) was a disgraceful error.**

Defiant was a failure against the Bf 109E. But seven days later remnants of 264 shot down "17 Messerschmitts without loss" and later on the same day destroyed eleven Ju 87s and 88s. Once the enemy were familiar with the Defiant it had had its day by daylight, but it did well in 1940–41 as a night fighter and was later fitted with radar. Most of the 1,064 built served as night fighters, target tugs and in air/sea rescue in Britain, the Middle East and Far East. Defiants carried the Mandrel jamming system to confuse German defences.

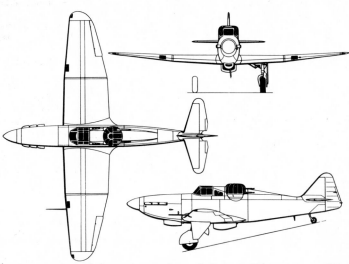

**Above: Defiant I (II similar) with turret fairings raised.**

# Bristol Type 156 Beaufighter

## Beaufighter I to TF.X (data mainly Mk X)

**Origin:** Bristol Aeroplane Company, Filton and Weston-Super-Mare; also Department of Aircraft Production, Australia.

**Type:** Two-seat torpedo strike fighter (other marks, night fighters, target tugs).

**Engines:** Two 1,770hp Bristol Hercules XVII 14-cylinder sleeve-valve radials; (Mk II) 1,250hp R-R Merlin XX; (other marks) different Hercules; (one-offs had R-R Griffons and Wright GR-2600 Cyclones).

**Dimensions:** Span 57ft 10in (17·63m); length 41ft 8in (12·6m) (II, 42ft 9in); height 15ft 10in (4·84m).

**Weights:** Empty 15,600lb (7100kg) (I, II, 13,800lb; VI, XI, 14,900lb); loaded 25,400lb (11,530kg) (most other marks 21,000lb, 9525kg).

**Performance:** Maximum speed 312mph (502km/h) (fighter marks, 330mph, 528km/h); initial climb 1,850ft (564m)/min; service ceiling 26,500ft (8077m) (fighters, 30,000ft, 9144m); range 1,540 miles (2478km).

**Armament:** Four 20mm Hispano cannon fixed in underside of forward fuselage (initially hand loaded with 60-round drums, later with belt feed), and one 0·303in Vickers K aimed by observer (fighters, also six 0·303in Brownings, two fixed in outer left wing and four in right. One 1,605lb (728kg) torpedo on centreline or 2,127lb (954kg) and wing racks for eight rocket projectiles or two 1,000lb (454kg) bombs.

**History:** First flight (Type 156 prototype) 17 July 1939; (production Mk I) May 1940; service delivery 27 July 1940; first flight (Mk 21, Australia) 26 May 1944; last delivery from new (UK) September 1945, (Australia) October 1945.

**Users:** Australia, Canada, New Zealand, South Africa, UK (RAF), US (AAF); other countries post-war.

**Development:** During the critical years 1935–39 the most glaring gap in the RAF's armoury was the lack of any long-range fighter, any cannon-armed fighter and any fighter capable of effective bomber escort and night

*Right: Seventh "Beau" built, a Mk IF of 25 Sqn at North Weald (before radar fitted).*

*Below: Typical Mk VIF, without AI.VIII radar, (probably) in Tunisia in 1942-43.*

fighting. Leslie Frise and engine designer Fedden talked at length of the possibility of creating a single type out of the Blenheim and Beaufort families that could meet all demands, but no official requirement was forth-coming — other than the strange F.11/37 Specification for a fighter with a heavily armed cannon turret. Eventually the two Bristol leaders did the obvious thing: they proposed a new twin-Hercules two-seater carrying enough armament to blast anything in front of it out of the sky. By using the wing, tail, landing gear, systems and jigs of the Beaufort it could be put into production quickly. The Air Ministry was enthusiastic and the first of what was to be an historic war-winning aeroplane took the air only six months later. A snub-nosed battleship, it was immensely strong, surprisingly manoeuvrable and a great basis for development. Almost its only operational shortcoming was a tendency to swing on takeoff or landing, and instability at low speeds, which later addition of a large dorsal fin and dihedral tailplane did not fully cure. ▶

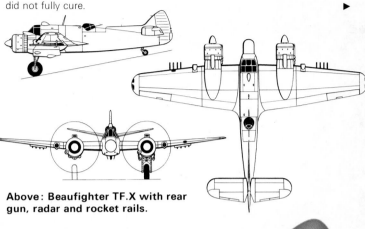

**Above:** Beaufighter TF.X with rear gun, radar and rocket rails.

► Early models barely exceeded 300mph with low-power Hercules and, in the absence of Griffon engines, 450 were fitted with Merlins, but these were less powerful and accentuated instability. Speed was soon judged less important when the need for night fighters to beat the Blitz became urgent. Equipped with AI Mk IV radar the early deliveries to 25 and 29 Sqns were a major reason for the Luftwaffe giving up the Blitz on Britain. Eventually the "Beau" served on all fronts, having thimble-nose AI Mk VII in 1942, tor-pedoes in 1943, rockets in 1944 and a spate of special installations in 1945. A total of 5,564 were built in England and 364 in Australia, the last fighter and torpedo versions serving with Coastal Command, the Far East Air Force and the RAAF until 1960. To the Luftwaffe it was a feared opponent even 500 miles out in the Atlantic; to the Japanese it was "Whispering death", so named because of the quietness of the sleeve-valve engines. It was sheer luck the "Beau" could be produced in time.

**Bristol Beaufighter I cutaway drawing key:**

1 Starboard navigation light (forward) and formation-keeping light (rear)
2 Wing structure
3 Aileron adjustable tab
4 Starboard aileron
5 Four Browning 0·303in machine guns
6 Machine gun ports
7 Starboard outer fuel tank (87 gal/395 litres)
8 Split trailing-edge flaps, hydraulically actuated
9 Fixed trailing edge
10 Flap operating jack
11 Starboard nacelle tail fairing
12 Oil tank (17 gal/77 litres)
13 Starboard inner fuel tank (188 gal/855 litres)
14 Cabin air duct
15 Hinged leading-edge for access
16 Engine bulkhead
17 Engine bearers
18 Auxiliary intake
19 Supercharger air intake
20 Cooling gills
21 Bristol Hercules III 14-cylinder sleeve-valve radial engine, 1,650 hp
22 De Havilland Hydromatic propeller
23 Spinner
24 Lockheed oleo-pneumatic shock-absorber
25 Starboard mainwheel, Dunlop brakes
26 Forward identification lamp in nose cap
27 Rudder pedals
28 Control column
29 Cannon ports
30 Seat adjusting lever
31 Pilot's seat
32 Instrument panel
33 Clear-vision panel
34 Flat bullet-proof windscreen
35 Fixed canopy (sideways-hinged on later aircraft)
36 Spar carry-through step
37 Nose/centre section attachment
38 Fuselage/centre section attachment
39 Pilot's entry/emergency escape hatchway
40 Underfloor cannon blast tubes
41 Fuselage/centre section attachment
42 Centre section attachment longeron reinforcement
43 Cabin air duct
44 Cannon heating duct
45 Rear spar carry-through
46 Bulkhead cut-out (observer access to front hatch)
47 Bulkhead
48 Hydraulic header tank
49 Aerial mast
50 Monocoque fuselage construction
51 Starboard cannon (two Hispano 20mm)
52 Floor level
53 Steps
54 Observer's swivel seat (normally forward-facing)
55 Radio controls and intercom
56 Observer's cupola
57 Hinged panel
58 Aerial
59 Oxygen bottles
60 Vertical control cable shaft
61 Sheet metal bulkhead
62 Control cables
63 Tailplane structure
64 Elevator
65 Elevator balance tab
66 Fin (extended forwards in dorsal fin on later aircraft)
67 Rudder balance
68 Rudder framework
69 Tail lights: formation-keeping (upper) and navigation (lower)
70 Rudder
71 Rudder trim tab
72 Elevator trim tab
73 Elevator balance tab
74 Elevator structure
75 Port tailplane (12 deg dihedral on later aircraft)
76 Rudder hinge (lower)
77 Tailwheel retraction mechanism
78 Retracting tailwheel
79 Tailwheel bay
80 Tail-unit joint ring
81 Control cables

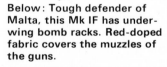

**Below: Tough defender of Malta, this Mk IF has under-wing bomb racks. Red-doped fabric covers the muzzles of the guns.**

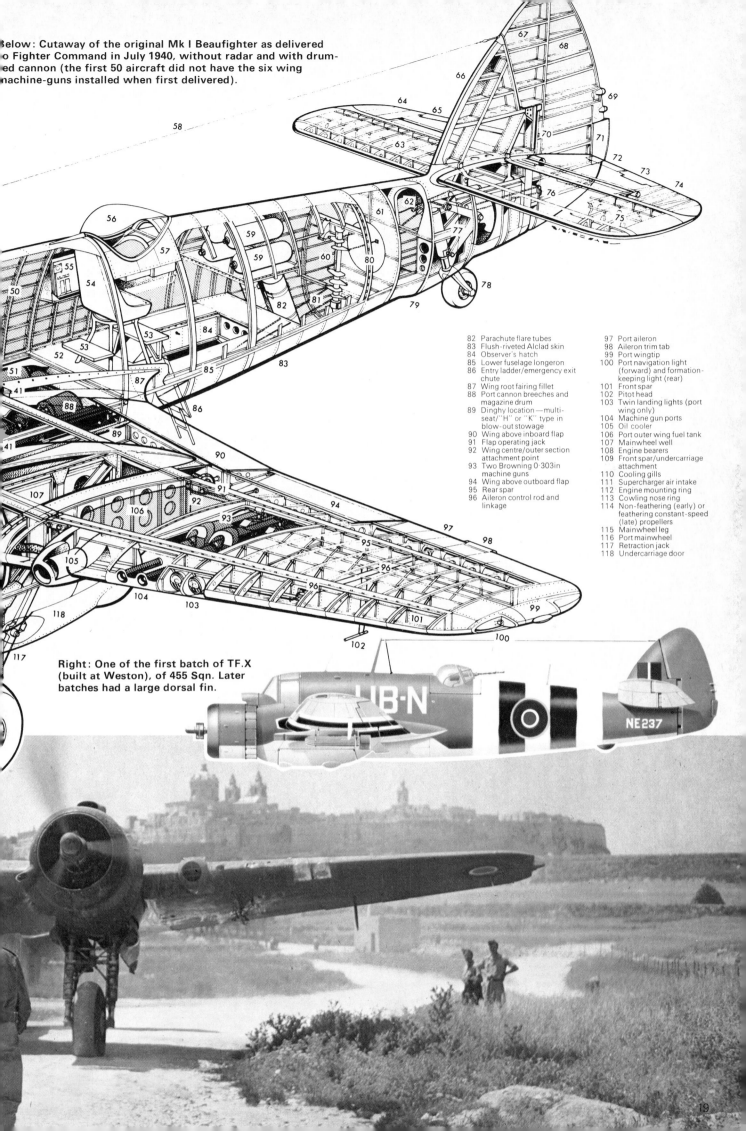

Below: Cutaway of the original Mk I Beaufighter as delivered to Fighter Command in July 1940, without radar and with drummed cannon (the first 50 aircraft did not have the six wing machine-guns installed when first delivered).

82 Parachute flare tubes
83 Flush-riveted Alclad skin
84 Observer's hatch
85 Lower fuselage longeron
86 Entry ladder/emergency exit chute
87 Wing root fairing fillet
88 Port cannon breeches and magazine drum
89 Dinghy location—multi-seat/"H" or "K" type in blow-out stowage
90 Wing above inboard flap
91 Flap operating jack
92 Wing centre/outer section attachment point
93 Two Browning 0·303in machine guns
94 Wing above outboard flap
95 Rear spar
96 Aileron control rod and linkage

97 Port aileron
98 Aileron trim tab
99 Port wingtip
100 Port navigation light (forward) and formation-keeping light (rear)
101 Front spar
102 Pitot head
103 Twin landing lights (port wing only)
104 Machine gun ports
105 Oil cooler
106 Port outer wing fuel tank
107 Mainwheel well
108 Engine bearers
109 Front spar/undercarriage attachment
110 Cooling gills
111 Supercharger air intake
112 Engine mounting ring
113 Cowling nose ring
114 Non-feathering (early) or feathering constant-speed (late) propellers
115 Mainwheel leg
116 Port mainwheel
117 Retraction jack
118 Undercarriage door

Right: One of the first batch of TF.X (built at Weston), of 455 Sqn. Later batches had a large dorsal fin.

19

# Bristol Type 152 Beaufort

## Beaufort I to VIII

**Origin:** Bristol Aeroplane Company; also made by Department of Aircraft Production, Fishermen's Bend, Australia.

**Type:** Four-seat torpedo bomber.

**Engines:** Two 1,130hp Bristol Taurus VI 14-cylinder sleeve-valve radials (most other marks, two 1,200hp Pratt & Whitney Twin Wasp).

**Dimensions:** Span 57ft 10in (17·63m); length 44ft 2in (13·46m); height 14ft 3in (4·34m).

**Weights:** Empty 13,107lb (5945kg); loaded 21,230lb (9629kg).

**Performance:** Maximum speed 260mph (418km/h) clean, 225mph (362km/h) with torpedo; service ceiling 16,500ft (5030m); range 1,600 miles (2575km).

**Armament:** Various, but typically two 0·303in Vickers K in dorsal turret and one fixed forward-firing in left wing, plus one 0·303in Browning in remote-control chin blister. Alternatively four 0·303in Brownings in wing, two Brownings manually aimed from beam windows and (Mk II) twin Brownings in dorsal turret (final 140 Australian Mk VIII, two 0·50in Brownings in dorsal turret). One 18in torpedo semi-external to left of centreline or bomb load of 2,000lb (907kg).

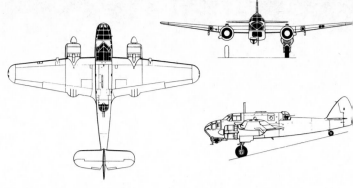

**Above: Three-view of Beaufort I Series II with trailing-edge extensions and rearward-firing barbette under the nose.**

**Below: Australian-built Beaufort VIII with Twin Wasp engines and increased-area fin. All served in the southwest Pacific.**

**Right: Beauforts in torpedo practice with 217 Sqn, Coastal Command (in 1940, before the grey/white colour scheme was introduced).**

**Below: A Beaufort II, with Twin Wasp engines, snug in one of the blast pens built at Luqa from Malta's bombed buildings. The unit is probably 86 Sqn, which replaced 217 in Malta when the original squadron flew to Burma.**

**History:** First flight 15 October 1938; first delivery October 1939; first flight of Australian aircraft (Mk V) August 1941; last delivery (Australia) August 1944.

**Users:** Australia, Turkey, UK.

**Development:** Derived from the Blenheim, the torpedo-carrying Beaufort was inevitably heavier because the Air Staff demanded a crew of four. Performance on Mercury engines was inadequate and, after studying an installation of the sleeve-valve Perseus, the choice fell on the Taurus, an extremely neat two-row engine only 46in in diameter. A clever installation was schemed for this but it overheated and various engine troubles held the programme back in the early days, but 22 and 42 Sqns of Coastal Command were fully operational by August 1940. As well as laying hundreds of mines they bombed the battlecruiser *Scharnhorst*, torpedoed the *Gneisenau* and sank numerous smaller ships. In 1939 plans were laid for Beaufort production in Australia and, because of the difficulty of supplying engines from Britain, the Australian Mks V–VIII had Twin Wasp engines, most of them made in Australia. A large batch of British Beauforts (Mk II) had this engine, but a Merlin-Beaufort was abandoned and from No 165 the Mk II reverted to later models of Taurus. The total built was 2,080, including 700 built in Australia for duty in the Southwest Pacific. Australian models had a bigger fin and progressed through four series with different equipment, ending with transport and trainer versions. The finest RAAF missions were against Japanese fleets at Normanby Island, in the Timor Sea and around New Guinea and the Solomons.

**Below: One of the first Mk I Beauforts to be delivered to 42 Sqn in early 1940. It has an early dorsal turret and under-nose gun but lacks the trailing edge extension-plates.**

# Bristol Type 142 Blenheim

## Types 142 M, 149 and 160 Blenheim/Bisley/Bolingbroke (data for Blenheim IVL)

**Origin:** Bristol Aeroplane Company; also made by A. V. Roe, Rootes Securities and Canadian Vickers Ltd.

**Type:** Three-seat light bomber (IF, IVF, fighter versions).

**Engines:** Two 920hp Bristol Mercury XV (I, Bolingbroke I, II, 840hp Mercury VIII; Bolingbroke IV series, 750–920hp Twin Wasp Junior, Cyclone or Mercury XX; Blenheim V, 950hp Mercury XXX).

**Dimensions:** Span 56ft 4in (17·17m) (V, 56ft 1in); length 42ft 9in (13m) (I, 39ft 9in; Bolingbroke III, 46ft 3in; V, 43ft 11in); height 12ft 10in (3·91m) (Bolingbroke III, 18ft).

**Weights:** Empty 9,790lb (4441kg) (I, Bolingbroke III, 8,700lb; V, 11,000lb); loaded 14,400lb (6531kg) (I, 12,250lb; Bolingbrokes 13,400lb; V, 17,000lb).

**Performance:** Maximum speed 266mph (428km/h); (I) 285mph; (early IV) 295mph; (Bolingbrokes and V) 245–260mph; initial climb 1,500ft (457m)/min (others similar); service ceiling 31,500ft (9600m) (others similar except Bolingbroke III, 26,000ft); range 1,950 miles (3138km); (I) 1,125 miles; (Bolingbrokes) 1,800 miles; (V) 1,600 miles.

**Armament:** One 0·303in Vickers K in nose, two 0·303in Brownings in FN.54 chin turret and two 0·303in Brownings in dorsal turret; (I) single fixed Browning and single Vickers K in dorsal turret; (IF, IVF) four fixed Brownings under fuselage; bomb load 1,000lb (454kg) internal (non-standard aircraft had underwing 500lb racks).

**History:** First flight (Type 142) 12 April 1935; (142M Blenheim I) 25 June 1936; service delivery November 1936; termination of production (VD) June 1943; withdrawal from service (Finland) 1956.

**Users:** Canada, Finland, France, Greece, Jugoslavia, Lithuania, Portugal, Romania, Turkey, UK (RAF).

**Development:** It was the newspaper magnate Lord Rothermere who asked the Bristol company to build him a fast executive aircraft to carry a

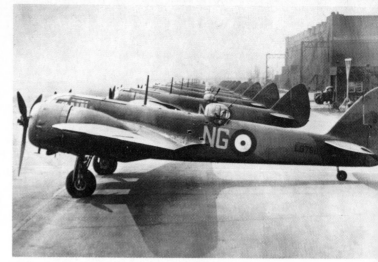

Above: Almost certainly taken at Northolt shortly after the start of World War II, this line-up of 604 (County of Middlesex) Sqn shows the Mk IF fighter. Soon this acquired the world's first airborne radar and operated mainly by night.

Below: A standard Blenheim I bomber of 60 Sqn, at Lahore, India. By 1940, the year relevant to this colour scheme, many Blenheims were being shipped out of England or withdrawn from operations.

Below: A trio of Blenheim IV bombers of 139 Sqn. On 3 September 1939 one of these was the first Allied aircraft to cross the German frontier in World War II. Before long, however, the Blenheim was found to be extremely vulnerable to modern fighters.

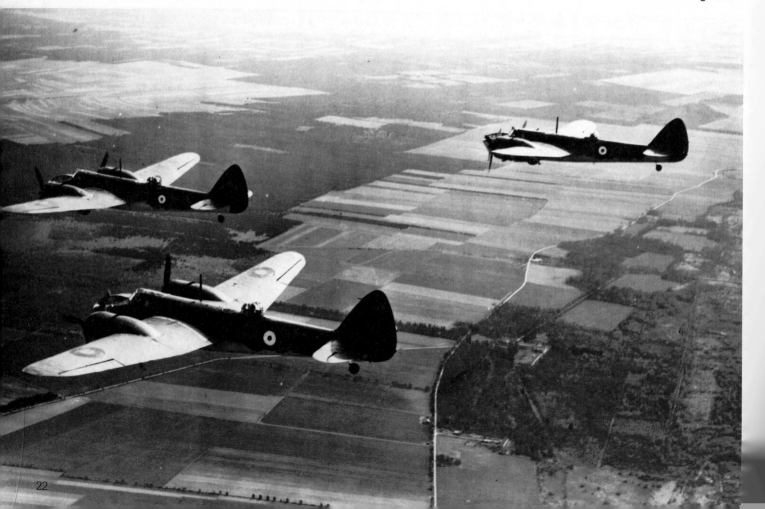

pilot and six passengers at 240mph, appreciably faster than any RAF fighter in 1934. The result was the Type 142, the first modern stressed-skin monoplane in Britain with retractable landing gear, flaps and, after a wait, imported American variable-pitch propellers. Its performance staggered even the designer, Barnwell, for on Air Ministry test it reached 307mph. The inevitable result was the Blenheim bomber, to produce which Barnwell designed a new fuselage with mid-wing and bomb bay beneath it. Pilot and nav/bomb-aimer sat in the neat glazed nose, and a part-retractable dorsal turret was added behind the wing. The Blenheim I was ordered in what were huge quantities to a company almost devoid of work. Ultimately 1,134 were built, many of which made gallant bombing raids early in the war and were then converted to IF fighter configuration (some having the AI Mk III, the first operational fighter radar in the world). The fast new bomber excited intense foreign interest and many were exported to Finland, Turkey, Jugoslavia, Lithuania, Romania and Greece. To provide a nav/bomb-aimer station ahead of the pilot the nose was then lengthened 3ft and this type was named Bolingbroke, a name retained for all the variety of Blenheims built in Canada (the Bolingbroke Mk III being a twin-float seaplane). A revised asymmetric nose was adopted for production in the speedy Mk IV, which later acquired a fighter gun pack (IVF) or a manual rear-firing chin gun (IVL), finally having a two-gun chin turret. Made by Bristol, Avro and Rootes, like the Mk I, the IV was the main combat version with the RAF, 3,297 being delivered and making many daylight missions in many theatres. The heavily armed and armoured two-seat Bisley attack aircraft did not go into production, but the three-seat equivalent did, as the Blenheim Mk V. Heavy and underpowered, the 902 VDs served in North Africa and the Far East.

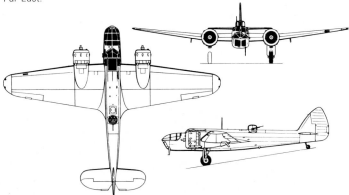

Above: Mk IV as originally delivered without under-nose gun.

Below: The "long-nosed" Blenheim IV, seen here in 1941, provided a proper station in the nose for the navigator/bomb-aimer. It carried more fuel than the Mk I, and needed more power.

Above: In the first two years of World War II British and other Allied aircraft were less effective against ships than such Luftwaffe aircraft as the Ju 87 and Ju 88. This Blenheim IV of 107 Sqn was photographed in June 1940 over a burning British ship off Bordeaux.

# De Havilland 82A Tiger Moth

## D.H.82 and 82A Tiger Moth I and II, PT-24

**Origin:** The de Havilland Aircraft Co, Hatfield; most UK production by Morris Motors, Cowley, and overseas production by DH Australia, DH Canada and DH New Zealand, with 200 assembled in Bombay.

**Type:** Primary trainer.

**Engine:** (I) 120hp DH Gipsy III inverted four-in-line, (II) 130hp Gipsy Major I.

**Dimensions:** Span 29ft 4in (8·94m); length (landplane) 23ft 11in (7·29m); height (landplane) 8ft 9½in (2·68m).

**Weights:** Empty 1,100–1,200lb (525kg); maximum (most) 1,825lb (828kg).

**Performance** (landplane): Maximum speed 109mph (175km/h); service ceiling 13,600ft (4150m); range 300 miles (482km).

**History:** First flight 26 October 1931; final delivery March 1945.

**Users:** (Wartime) Australia, Canada, Egypt, Iran, Iraq, New Zealand, Portugal, S Africa, S Rhodesia, UK (RAF, RN), Uruguay, USA (USAAF).

Above: Tiger Moth II (early series) with fuselage bomb rack.

**Development:** The original Moth of 1925 was developed into the Gipsy Moth and Genet Moth, both used as standard RAF elementary trainer and liaison aircraft, and then into the Tiger Moth with airframe of a different shape ideally suited for military training with seat-type parachute. Fully aerobatic, the Tiger was used for all ab.initio pilot training and in a few cases (eg, in Iraq) carried armament. Total production amounted to 1,611 pre-war, 795 wartime at Hatfield, 3,210 by Morris, 1,520 in Canada, 1,085 in Australia and 344 in New Zealand. A few had floats, and many Canadian Tigers had heated enclosed cockpits and skis (USAAF designation PT-24). Nearly all Tigers were of the more powerful Mk II type, and in 1940 anti-spin strakes were added ahead of the tailplane roots. For a few weeks in 1940 a considerable number were flown by EFTS instructors on armed coastal patrol around Britain. Tigers continued in service in many air forces into the 1950s.

### DE HAVILLAND QUEEN BEE (DH.82B)

First flown in 1935, this radio-controlled target was derived from the Tiger Moth by fitting a new all-wood fuselage with only the front cockpit. A few were seaplanes, and by 1944 Hatfield had built 320 and Scottish Aviation 60 for the RAF and Fleet Air Arm for use as targets for AA gunnery and in research programmes.

Left: This Tiger Moth II is typical of the early wartime aircraft, without extended tailplane-root strakes. In 1940 there was fear of German gas attack, and British service aircraft had a square or triangle of special paint, usually ahead of the fin (but sometimes on the fin itself) which changed colour in presence of gas.

Below: This later Mk II, with tailplane-root strakes, is being used for practice bombing in the post-1942 era—in the author's experience, most unusual. EM836, built by Morris Motors at Cowley, is fitted with a blind-flying hood over the rear cockpit and has a training-yellow side stripe.

# De Havilland 98 Mosquito

## D.H.98 Mosquito I to 43

**Origin:** The de Havilland Aircraft Company, Hatfield and Leavesden; also built by Airspeed, Percival Aircraft and Standard Motors (Canley); de Havilland Aircraft Pty, Australia; de Havilland Aircraft of Canada.

**Type:** Designed as high-speed day bomber, see text for subsequent variants.

**Engines:** (Mks II, III, IV and early VI) two 1,230hp Rolls-Royce Merlin 21 or (late FB.VI) 1,635hp Merlin 25; (Mk IX) 1,680hp Merlin 72; (Mk XVI) Merlin 72 or 1,710hp Merlin 73 or 77; (Mk 30) 1,710hp Merlin 76; (Mk 33) 1,640hp Merlin 25; (Mks 34, 35, 36) 1,690hp Merlin 113/114. Many other variants had corresponding Merlins made by Packard.

**Dimensions:** Span (except Mk XV) 54ft 2in (16·5m); length (most common) 40ft 6in (12·34m); (bombers) 40ft 9½in; (radar-equipped fighters and Mks 34–38) typically 41ft 9in; (Mk 39) 43ft 4in; height (most common) 15ft 3½in (4·66m).

**Weights:** Empty (Mks II–VI) about 14,100lb; (Mks VIII–30) about 15,200lb; (beyond Mk 30) about 15,900–16,800lb; maximum gross (Mks II and III) around 17,500lb; (Mks IV and VI) about 22,500lb; (later night fighters) about 20,500lb (but HF.XV only 17,395lb); (Mks IX, XVI and marks beyond 30) typically 25,000lb (11,340kg).

**Performance:** Maximum speed, from 300mph (TT.39 with M4 sleeve) to 370mph (595km/h) for early night fighters, 380mph (612km/h) for III, IV and VI, 410mph (660km/h) for IX, XVI and 30, and 425mph for 34 and 35; service ceiling, from 30,000ft (9144m) for low-rated naval versions to 34,500ft (10,520m) for most marks, to around 40,000ft (12,190m) for high-blown versions, with Mk XV reaching 44,000ft (13,410m); combat range, typically 1,860 miles (2990km), with naval TFs down at 1,260 miles and PR.34 up to 3,500 miles.

**Armament:** See text.

**History:** See text.

**Users:** Australia, Belgium, Canada, China, Czechoslovakia, France, Jugoslavia, New Zealand, Norway, Soviet Union, Turkey, UK (RAF, RN, BOAC), US (AAF).

▶

**Right:** An FB.VI, the most numerous single mark, attacking a ship in 1944. Cannon were used to help sight the eight rockets, which appear to have hit ideally below the waterline.

**Below:** A B.IV of 139 Sqn (the second user) at Marham, 1942.

**Below:** Almost certainly taken at Swanton Morley in early 1942, this scene shows quartets of 500-pounders— then all the "Mossie" could carry—going aboard a 105 Sqn B.IV.

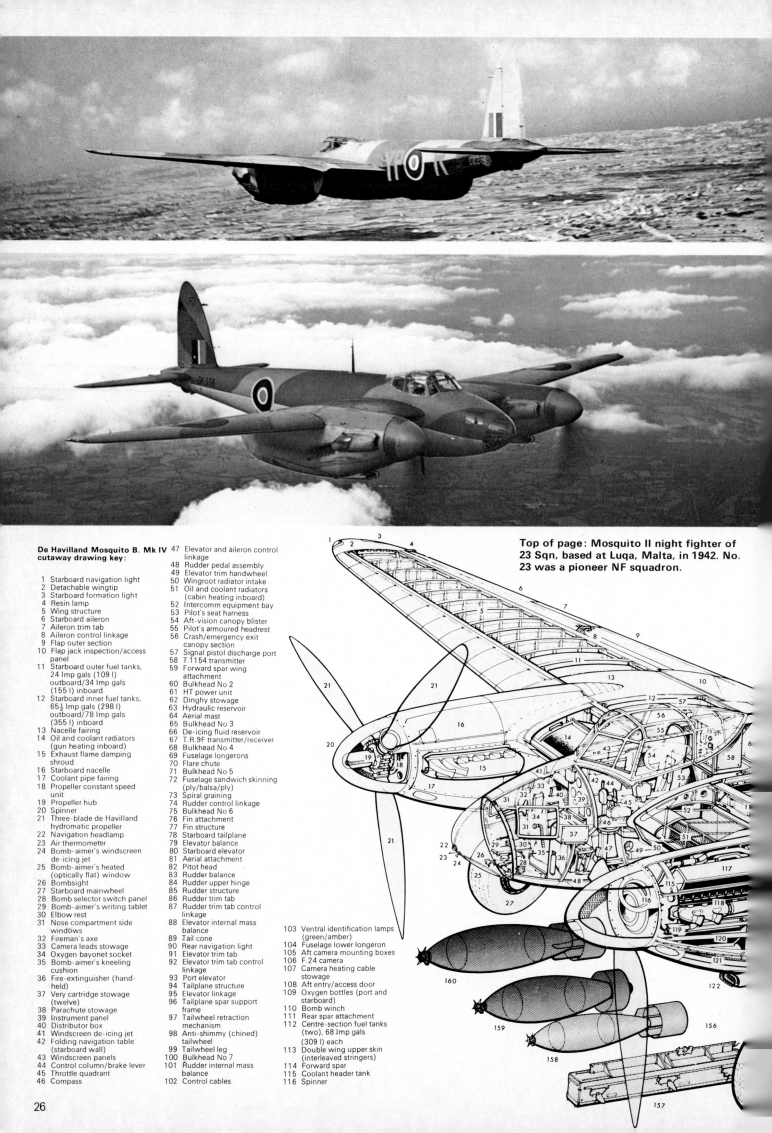

**De Havilland Mosquito B. Mk IV cutaway drawing key:**

1 Starboard navigation light
2 Detachable wingtip
3 Starboard formation light
4 Resin lamp
5 Wing structure
6 Starboard aileron
7 Aileron trim tab
8 Aileron control linkage
9 Flap outer section
10 Flap jack inspection/access panel
11 Starboard outer fuel tanks, 24 Imp gals (109 l) outboard/34 Imp gals (155 l) inboard
12 Starboard inner fuel tanks, 65½ Imp gals (298 l) outboard/78 Imp gals (355 l) inboard
13 Nacelle fairing
14 Oil and coolant radiators (gun heating inboard)
15 Exhaust flame damping shroud
16 Starboard nacelle
17 Coolant pipe fairing
18 Propeller constant speed unit
19 Propeller hub
20 Spinner
21 Three-blade de Havilland hydromatic propeller
22 Navigation headlamp
23 Air thermometer
24 Bomb-aimer's windscreen de-icing jet
25 Bomb-aimer's heated (optically flat) window
26 Bombsight
27 Starboard mainwheel
28 Bomb selector switch panel
29 Bomb-aimer's writing tablet
30 Elbow rest
31 Nose compartment side windows
32 Fireman's axe
33 Camera leads stowage
34 Oxygen bayonet socket
35 Bomb-aimer's kneeling cushion
36 Fire-extinguisher (hand-held)
37 Very cartridge stowage (twelve)
38 Parachute stowage
39 Instrument panel
40 Distributor box
41 Windscreen de-icing jet
42 Folding navigation table (starboard wall)
43 Windscreen panels
44 Control column/brake lever
45 Throttle quadrant
46 Compass

47 Elevator and aileron control linkage
48 Rudder pedal assembly
49 Elevator trim handwheel
50 Wingroot radiator intake
51 Oil and coolant radiators (cabin heating inboard)
52 Intercomm equipment bay
53 Pilot's seat harness
54 Aft-vision canopy blister
55 Pilot's armoured headrest
56 Crash/emergency exit canopy section
57 Signal pistol discharge port
58 T.1154 transmitter
59 Forward spar wing attachment
60 Bulkhead No 2
61 HT power unit
62 Dinghy stowage
63 Hydraulic reservoir
64 Aerial mast
65 Bulkhead No 3
66 De-icing fluid reservoir
67 T.R.9F transmitter/receiver
68 Bulkhead No 4
69 Fuselage longerons
70 Flare chute
71 Bulkhead No 5
72 Fuselage sandwich skinning (ply/balsa/ply)
73 Spiral graining
74 Rudder control linkage
75 Bulkhead No 6
76 Fin attachment
77 Fin structure
78 Starboard tailplane
79 Elevator balance
80 Starboard elevator
81 Aerial attachment
82 Pitot head
83 Rudder balance
84 Rudder upper hinge
85 Rudder structure
86 Rudder trim tab
87 Rudder trim tab control linkage
88 Elevator internal mass balance
89 Tail cone
90 Rear navigation light
91 Elevator trim tab
92 Elevator trim tab control linkage
93 Port elevator
94 Tailplane structure
95 Elevator linkage
96 Tailplane spar support frame
97 Tailwheel retraction mechanism
98 Anti-shimmy (chined) tailwheel
99 Tailwheel leg
100 Bulkhead No 7
101 Rudder internal mass balance
102 Control cables

103 Ventral identification lamps (green/amber)
104 Fuselage lower longeron
105 Aft camera mounting boxes
106 F.24 camera
107 Camera heating cable stowage
108 Aft entry/access door
109 Oxygen bottles (port and starboard)
110 Bomb winch
111 Rear spar attachment
112 Centre-section fuel tanks (two), 68 Imp gals (309 l) each
113 Double wing upper skin (interleaved stringers)
114 Forward spar
115 Coolant header tank
116 Spinner

**Top of page:** Mosquito II night fighter of 23 Sqn, based at Luqa, Malta, in 1942. No. 23 was a pioneer NF squadron.

**Development:** The de Havilland Aircraft Co planned the Mosquito in October 1938 as a high-speed unarmed day bomber, with the added attraction of wooden construction to ease the strain on Britain's hard-pressed materials suppliers. The Air Ministry showed no interest, suggesting instead the Hatfield plant should make wings for existing heavy bombers. In 1940, with extreme reluctance, it was agreed to allow the firm to proceed, the only role thought possible for an unarmed aircraft being reconnaissance. The first prototype, built secretly at Salisbury Hall by a team which grew from 12 in January 1940 to 30 in the summer, was flown painted yellow on 25 November 1940. From it stemmed 7,781 aircraft, built in Britain, Canada and Australia, of the following types;

PR.I Unarmed photo-reconnaissance, with span lengthened from 52ft 6in of prototype to 54ft 2in but still with short engine nacelles.

F.II Night fighter, with pilot and observer side by side, flat bullet-proof windscreen, extended nacelles (as in all subsequent aircraft, with flaps divided into inner and outer segments) and armament of four 20mm Hispano cannon with 300 rounds each under the floor and four 0·303in Brownings with 2,000 rounds each in the nose. First flew 15 May 1941; subsequently fitted with AI Mk IV or V radar or Turbinlight searchlight.

T.III Dual-control trainer, first flown January 1942 but produced mainly after the war (last delivery 1949).

B.IV Unarmed bomber, carrying four 500lb (227kg) bombs internally; first delivered to 105 Sqn at Swanton Morley November 1941, making first operational sortie (Cologne, the morning after the first 1,000-bomber night attack) on 31 May 1942. Some later fitted with bulged bomb bays for 4,000lb (1814kg) bomb.

FB.VI Fighter-bomber and intruder, by day or night; same guns as F.II but two 250lb (113kg) bombs in rear bay and two more (later two 500lb) on wing racks; alternatively, 50 or 100 gal drop tanks, mines, depth charges or eight 60lb rockets. Some fitted with AI radar. Total production 2,584, more than any other mark.

B.VII Canadian-built Mk IV, used in North America only.

PR.VIII Reconnaissance conversion of B.IV with high-blown Merlin 61.

Mk IX Important advance in bomber (B.IX) and reconnaissance (PR.IX) versions; high-blown two-stage engines, bulged bomb bay for 4,000lb bomb or extra fuel, much increased weight, paddle-blade propellers and new avionics (Rebecca, Boozer, Oboe or $H_2S$ Mk VI).

NF.XII Conversion of F.II fitted with new thimble nose containing AI Mk VIII centimetric radar in place of Brownings.

NF.XIII Similar to Mk XII but built as new, with thimble or bull nose and same wing as Mk VI for drop tanks or other stores; flew August 1943.

NF.XV High-altitude fighter with wings extended to 59ft, pressurised cockpit, lightened structure, AI Mk VIII in nose and belly pack of four 0·303in Brownings to combat Ju 86P raiders.

Mk XVI Further major advance with two-stage Merlins, bulged bomb bay and pressurised cockpit. PR.XVI flew July 1943; B.XVI in January 1944, over 1,200 of latter being used for high-level nuisance raids with 4,000lb bombs.

NF.XVII Night fighter with new AI Mk X or SCR.720 (some with tail-looking scanner also); four 20mm each with 500 rounds.

FB.XVIII Dubbed Tse-Tse Fly, this multi-role Coastal Command fighter had low-blown engines and carried a 57mm six-pounder Molins gun with 25 rounds plus four Brownings, as well as eight 60lb rockets or bombs.

NF.XIX Mk XIII developed with AI.VIII or X or SCR.720 in bulged Universal Nose and low-blown Merlin 25s.

B.XX Canadian-built B.IV (USAAF designation F-8).

FB.21 to T.29, Canadian marks with Packard V-1650 (Merlin) engines, not all built.

NF.30 Night fighter with two-stage engines, paddle blades, AI Mk X and various sensing, spoofing or jamming avionics; based on Mk XIX.

PR.32 Extended-span reconnaissance version with Merlin 113/114.

Mk 33 First Royal Navy Sea Mosquito version, with power-folding wings, oleo main legs (in place of rubber in compression), low-blown engines driving four-blade propellers, arrester hook, four 20mm cannon, torpedo (or various bomb/rocket loads), American ASH radar and rocket JATO boost.

PR.34 Strategic reconnaissance version, with 113/114 engines, extra-bulged belly for 1,269 gal fuel (200gal drop tanks) and pressure cabin.

B.35 Equivalent bomber version, with PR and target-tug offshoots.

NF.36 Postwar fighter, with 113/114 engines and AI Mk X.

TF.37 Naval torpedo-fighter; basically Mk 33 with AI/ASV Mk XIII.

NF.38 Final fighter, mainly exported; AI Mk IX, forward cockpit.

TT.39 Complete rebuild by General Aircraft as specialised target tug.

FB.40 Australian-built Mk VI, with PR.40 as conversions.

PR.41 Australian-built derivative of PR.IX and Mk 40.

T.43 Australian trainer; all Australian production had Packard engines.

**Facing page, lower:** One of the first batch of Mk IV bomber Mosquitoes. Though slower than prototypes of later fighters, they were the fastest aircraft in service in 1941.

**Left:** Cutaway drawing of a typical Mk IV, the original bomber version that entered squadron service in November 1941, within a year of first flight. Subsequently the bomb load was doubled.

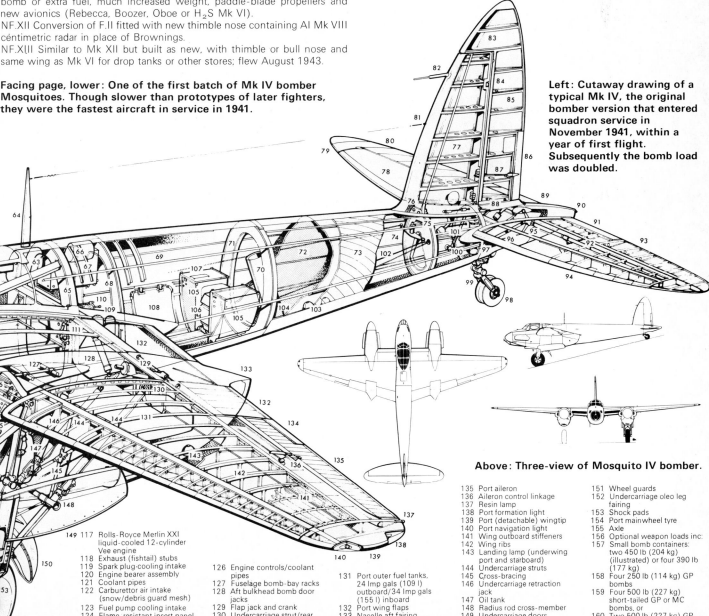

**Above: Three-view of Mosquito IV bomber.**

117 Rolls-Royce Merlin XXI liquid-cooled 12-cylinder Vee engine
118 Exhaust (fishtail) stubs
119 Spark plug-cooling intake
120 Engine bearer assembly
121 Coolant pipes
122 Carburettor air intake (snow/debris guard mesh)
123 Fuel pump cooling intake
124 Flame-resistant insert panel
125 Engine accessories
126 Engine controls/coolant pipes
127 Fuselage bomb-bay racks
128 Aft bulkhead bomb door jacks
129 Flap jack and crank
130 Undercarriage strut/rear spar attachment
131 Port outer fuel tanks, 24 Imp gals (109 l) outboard/34 Imp gals (155 l) inboard
132 Port wing flaps
133 Nacelle aft fairing
134 Aileron trim tab
135 Port aileron
136 Aileron control linkage
137 Resin lamp
138 Port formation light
139 Port (detachable) wingtip
140 Port navigation light
141 Wing outboard stiffeners
142 Wing ribs
143 Landing lamp (underwing port and starboard)
144 Undercarriage struts
145 Cross-bracing
146 Undercarriage retraction jack
147 Oil tank
148 Radius rod cross-member
149 Undercarriage doors
150 Mudguard
151 Wheel guards
152 Undercarriage oleo leg fairing
153 Shock pads
154 Port mainwheel tyre
155 Axle
156 Optional weapon loads inc:
157 Small bomb containers: two 450 lb (204 kg) (illustrated) or four 390 lb (177 kg)
158 Four 250 lb (114 kg) GP bombs
159 Four 500 lb (227 kg) short-tailed GP or MC bombs, or
160 Two 500 lb (227 kg) GP bombs

# Fairey Albacore

## Albacore I

**Origin:** Fairey Aviation Co, Hayes and Hamble.
**Type:** Carrier torpedo bomber.
**Engine:** 1,065hp Bristol Taurus II 14-cylinder sleeve-valve radial or 1,130hp Taurus XII.
**Dimensions:** Span 50ft 0in (15·24m); length 39ft 9½in (12·13m); height 15ft 3in (4·65m).
**Weights:** Empty 7,250lb (3289kg); maximum 10,600lb (4808kg).
**Performance:** Maximum speed 161mph (259km/h); service ceiling 20,700ft (6309m); range 930 miles (1497km).
**Armament:** Two 0·303in Vickers K manually aimed from rear cockpit, sometimes 0·303in Browning in lower right wing; 1,610lb (730kg) torpedo or up to 2,000lb (907kg) bombs.
**History:** First flight 12 December 1938; service delivery December 1939; combat service March 1940; final delivery May 1943.
**User:** Canada (RCAF), UK (RN).

**Development:** Planned as a successor to the Swordfish, the Albacore was designed to specification S.41/36. Though still a biplane, with wings braced with wire and covered with fabric, it had an all-metal monocoque fuselage and heated enclosed cabin. Pilot view was superb, and the "Applecore" was in fact very pleasant to fly. Fairey built 803, and though this was only a quarter of the number of Swordfish built (which stayed in production at Blackburn to the end of the war) the Albacore saw intense

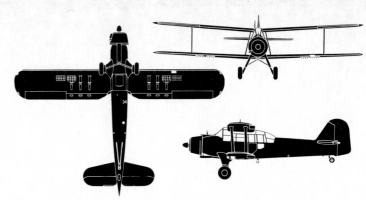

Above: Albacore I with multiple underwing stores racks.

Right: BF759, an Albacore I (the only mark, though there were many detail differences). It is apparently carrying mines on the wing racks, and the flaps are down.

action from the Arctic to Malaya. The first major torpedo attack was at Cape Matapan in March 1941; by 1942 there were 15 FAA squadrons, several of them shore-based in North Africa. Missions included target marking with flares, close support of troops with bombs, minelaying of European harbours and sinking flak-bristling E-boats from mast height. But it never became famous.

# Fairey Barracuda

## Type 100 Barracuda I, II, III and V

**Origin:** The Fairey Aviation Company; also built by Blackburn Aircraft, Boulton Paul Aircraft and Westland Aircraft.
**Type:** Three-seat (Mk V, two-seat) naval torpedo/dive bomber.
**Engine:** (I) one 1,260hp Rolls-Royce Merlin 30 vee-12 liquid-cooled; (II and III) one 1,640hp Merlin 32; (V) one 2,020hp R-R Griffon 37.
**Dimensions:** Span (I-III) 49ft 2in (15m); (V) 53ft 0in (16·15m); length (I-III) 39ft 9in (12·12m); (V) 41ft 1in (12·5m); height (I-III) 15ft 1in (4·6m); (V) 13ft 2in (4m).
**Weights:** Empty (I) 8,700lb (3946kg); (II, III) 9,407lb (4267kg); (V) 9,800lb (4445kg); loaded (I) 13,500lb (6125kg); (II, III) 14,100lb (6395kg); (V) 16,400lb (7450kg).
**Performance:** Maximum speed (I) 235mph; (II) 228mph (367km/h); (III) 239mph; (V) 264mph (422km/h); initial climb (I-III) 950ft (290m)/min; (V) 2,000ft (610m)/min; service ceiling (I) 18,400ft; (II) 16,600ft (5060m); (III) 20,000ft (6096m); (V) 24,000ft; range with full weapon load, (I, II) 524 miles (845km); (III)·686 miles (1104km); (V) 600 miles.
**Armament:** (I-III) two 0·303in Vickers K manually aimed in rear cockpit; (V) one fixed 0·50in Browning in wing, no rear guns; one 18in torpedo (1,610 or 1,620lb) or bomb load up to 2,000lb (907kg) under fuselage and wings (including mines or depth charges).
**History:** First flight 7 December 1940; production Mk I, 18 May 1942; service delivery, 10 January 1943; first Mk V (converted II) 16 November 1944; final delivery January 1946.
**User:** UK (RN).

**Development:** The Barracuda was designed to Specification S.24/37 to replace the Albacore, which in turn had been designed to replace the venerable Swordfish. The Albacore was withdrawn from production in 1943, after 800 had been built, while manufacture of Swordfish continued. The Barracuda, however, was in a different class and might have played a greater part in World War II had it not been so severely delayed. The first delay, from 1938–40, was due to abandonment of the proposed Rolls-Royce Exe engine, and the low-rated Merlin was only marginally powerful enough

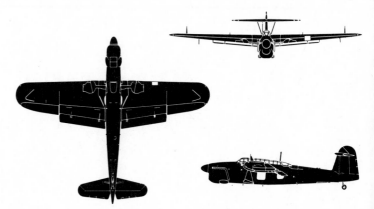

Above: Three-view of Barracuda II, without ASV radar.

as a substitute. Pressure of other programmes held back production two further years, but in May 1943 No 827 Sqn, Fleet Air Arm, was fully equipped and in April 1944 *Victorious* and *Furious* sent 42 aircraft to Kaafjord, Norway, to score 15 direct hits on the *Tirpitz* (for the loss of only two aircraft) in steep dive-bombing with armour-piercing bombs. Later the same month Barracudas were in heavy actions in the Dutch East Indies, and others were equipped to para-drop secret agents (from underwing nacelles) to occupied Europe. The II had more power and four-blade propeller, later receiving ASV.IIN radar, while the III had ASV.10 in an under-fuselage radome. Wartime output of "Barras" was: Fairey 1,131, Blackburn 700, Boulton Paul 692 and Westland 18 (mostly IIs). In 1945 production began on the much more powerful Mk V, later called TF.5, with redesigned structure and accommodation. Radar was housed in a left-wing pod, and later Mk Vs had a tall pointed tail and other changes, but only 30 were built and used mainly for training.

Below: A Barracuda II of a late batch fitted with ASV.IIN radar. Though curious in layout, and underpowered, the "Barra" proved effective in numerous difficult roles.

# Fairey Battle

## Battle I to IV (data for II)

**Origin:** The Fairey Aviation Company; and Avions Fairey, Belgium; shadow production by Austin Motors.
**Type:** Three-seat light bomber.
**Engine:** One 1,030hp Rolls-Royce Merlin II vee-12 liquid-cooled.
**Dimensions:** Span 54ft 0in (16·46m); length 42ft 1¾in (12·85m); height 15ft 6in (4·72m).
**Weights:** Empty 6,647lb (3015kg); loaded 10,792lb (4895kg).
**Performance:** Maximum speed 241mph (388km/h); initial climb 920ft (280m)/min; service ceiling 25,000ft (7620m); range with bomb load at economical setting 900 miles (1448km).
**Armament:** One 0·303in Browning fixed in right wing and one 0·303in Vickers K manually aimed in rear cockpit; bomb load up to 1,000lb (454kg) in four cells in inner wings.
**History:** First flight (prototype) 10 March 1936; production Mk I, June 1937; final delivery January 1941; withdrawal from service 1949.
**User:** Australia, Belgium, Canada, Poland, South Africa, Southern Rhodesia, Turkey, UK (RAF).

**Development:** The Battle will forever be remembered as a combat aeroplane which seemed marvellous when it appeared and yet which, within four years, was being hacked out of the sky in droves so that, ever afterward, aircrew think of the name with a shudder. There was nothing faulty about the aircraft; it was simply a sitting duck for modern fighters. Designed to Specification P.27/32 as a replacement for the biplane Hart and Hind, this clean cantilever stressed-skin monoplane epitomised modern design and carried twice the bomb load for twice the distance at 50 per cent higher speed. It was the first aircraft to go into production with the new Merlin engine, taking its mark number (I, II, III or IV) from that of the engine. Ordered in what were previously unheard-of quantities (155, then 500 and then 863 from a new Austin 'shadow factory'), production built up faster than for any other new British aircraft; 15 RAF bomber squadrons were equipped between May 1937 and May 1938. When World War II began, more than 1,000 were in service and others were exported to Poland, Turkey and Belgium (where 18 were built by Avions Fairey). On 2 September 1939 ten Battle squadrons flew to France as the major offensive element of the Advanced Air Striking Force. They were plunged into furious fighting from 10 May 1940 and suffered grievously. On the first day of the Blitzkrieg in the West two members of 12 Sqn won posthumous VCs and four days later, in an all-out attack on German pontoon bridges at Sedan, 71 Battles attacked and 31 returned. Within six months all Battles were being replaced in front-line units and the survivors of the 2,419 built were shipped to Canada or Australia as trainers (many with separate instructor/pupil cockpits) or used as target tugs or test beds.

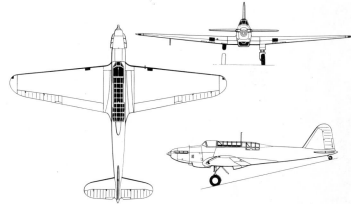

**Above: Three-view of a standard Battle bomber (Mks I to IV).**

**Above: Flap position suggests this Battle has just landed. The yellow roundel ring was added to most Battles after the débacle in France, where the usual roundel was equal radii red, white and blue, often with striped rudder (not fin).**

**Below: One of the original batch of 150 Battle Is built at Stockport, seen with 106 Sqn in 1937 markings. Light series bomb carriers were usually under the wing.**

# Fairey Firefly

## Firefly I to 7 and U.8 to 10

**Origin:** The Fairey Aviation Company.
**Type:** Originally two-seat naval fighter; later, see text.
**Engine:** I, up to No 470, one 1,730hp Rolls-Royce Griffon IIB vee-12 liquid-cooled; from No 471, 1,990hp Griffon XII; Mks 4–7, 2,245hp Griffon 74.
**Dimensions:** Span (I-III) 44ft 6in (13·55m), (4-6) 41ft 2in (12·55m), (7) 44ft 6in (13·55m); length (I-III) 37ft 7in (11·4m); (4-6) 37ft 11in (11·56m); (7) 38ft 3in (11·65m); height (I-III) 13ft 7in (4·15m); (4-7) 14ft 4in (4·37m).
**Weights:** Empty (I) 9,750lb (4422kg); (4) 9,900lb (4491kg); (7) 11,016lb (4997kg); loaded (I) 14,020lb (6359kg); (4) 13,927lb (6317kg) clean, 16,096lb (7301kg) with external stores; (7) 13,970lb (6337kg).
**Performance:** Maximum speed (I) 316mph (509km/h); (4) 386mph (618km/h); initial climb (I) 1,700ft (518m)/min; (4) 2,050ft (625m)/min; service ceiling (I) 28,000ft (8534m); (4) 31,000ft (9450m); range on internal fuel (I) 580 miles (933km); (4) 760 miles (1223km).
**Armament:** (I) four fixed 20mm Hispano cannon in wings; underwing racks for up to 2,000lb (907kg) of weapons or other stores; (4 and 5) usually similar to I in most sub-types; (6) no guns, but underwing load increased to 3,000lb and varied; (7) no guns, but underwing load remained at 3,000lb and equipment changed.
**History:** First flight 22 December 1941; first production F.I 26 August

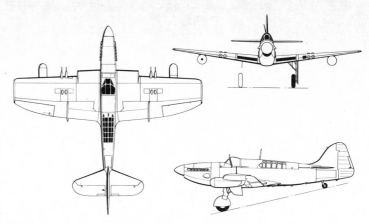

**Above: Three-view of Fairey Firefly FR.5.**

1942; production FR.4, 25 May 1945; final delivery of new aircraft May 1955.
**User:** UK (RN); other countries post-war.

**Development:** Before World War II Fairey designed a light bomber, P.4/34, from which evolved the Fulmar naval two-seat fighter to Specification O.8/38. A total of 600 of these slender carrier-based aircraft served during the war with various equipment and roles. The Firefly followed the same formula, but was much more powerful and useful. Designed to N.5/40 — a merger of N.8/39 and N.9/39 — it was a clean stressed-skin machine with folding elliptical wings housing the four cannon and with the trailing edge provided with patented Youngman flaps for use at low speeds and in cruise. Unlike the installation on the Barracuda, these flaps could be recessed into the wing. The pilot sat over the leading edge, with the observer behind the wing. The main wartime version was the Mk I, widely used from the end of 1943 in all theatres. Fairey and General Aircraft built 429 F.Is, 376 FR.Is with ASH radar and then 37 NF.2 night fighters. There followed the more powerful Mk III, from which derived the redesigned FR.4 with two-stage Griffon and wing-root radiators. There were 160 of these, 40 going to the Netherlands and the rest serving in Korea, with the 352 Mk 5s with folding wings. There were FR, NF and AS (anti-submarine) Mk 5s, and they were followed by the 133 specialised AS.6 versions with all role equipment tailored to anti-submarine operations. The 151 AS.7s rounded off production, this being a redesigned three-seater, with new tail and wings and distinctive beard radiator. More than 400 Fireflies were rebuilt in the 1950s as two-cockpit T.1s or armed T.2s, or as various remotely piloted drone versions (U.8, U.9, U.10). Some were converted as target tugs and for other civil duties.

**Left: The wartime marks of Firefly had manually folded wings. These Firefly F.Is are being recovered after a Pacific mission.**

---

# Fairey Fulmar

## Fulmar I and II

**Origin:** Fairey Aviation Co, Hayes.
**Type:** Carrier fighter bomber.
**Engine:** (I) 1,080hp Rolls-Royce Merlin VIII vee-12 liquid-cooled; (II) 1,300hp Merlin 30.
**Dimensions:** Span 46ft 4½in (14·14m); length 40ft 2in (12·24m); height 10ft 8in (3·25m).
**Weights:** Empty (II) 7,015lb (3182kg); normal loaded (II) 9,672lb (4387kg); maximum 10,200lb (4627kg).
**Performance:** Maximum speed (II) 272mph (440km/h); service ceiling (II) 27,200ft (8300m); range 780 miles (1255km).
**Armament:** Eight 0·303in Browning fixed in outer wings (some also 0·303in Vickers K manually aimed from rear cockpit), with underwing racks for two 250lb (113kg) bombs.
**History:** First flight 4 January 1940; service delivery 10 May 1940.
**User:** UK (RN).

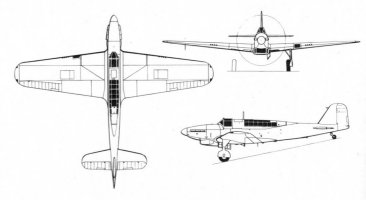

**Above: Three-view of Fairey Fulmar I.**

**Development:** Based on the P.4/34 light bomber first flown in January 1937, the Fulmar was designed by a team under Marcel O. Lobelle to meet the Admiralty's urgent need for a modern shipboard fighter. Specification O.8/38 was drawn up around the Fairey design, stipulating eight guns and a seat for a navigator. Development and clearance for service was amazingly rapid, and 806 Sqn equipped with the new fighter in July, reaching the Mediterranean aboard *Illustrious* in August 1940. Later 14 FAA squadrons used the Fulmar, most seeing intensive action in the Mediterranean or aboard CAM (catapult-armed merchant) ships in Atlantic convoys (a Fulmar was shot from a CAM ship as early as August 1941). Against the Regia Aeronautica the Fulmar did well, having adequate performance, good handling and fair endurance. After building 250 Mk I Fairey delivered 350 of the more powerful Mk II, the last in February 1943.

**Left: N1854, the prototype Fulmar. This two-seat naval fighter was in service within weeks of its first taking the air.**

# Fairey Swordfish

## Swordfish I-IV

**Origin:** The Fairey Aviation Company; later Blackburn Aircraft.
**Type:** Basic role, two-seat torpedo carrier and three-seat spotter reconnaissance; later many other duties.
**Engine:** (Mk I and early II) one 690hp Bristol Pegasus IIIM3 nine-cylinder radial; (later II onwards) 750hp Pegasus 30.
**Dimensions:** Span 45ft 6in (13·87m); length (landplane) 35ft 8in (10·87m); height 12ft 4in (3·76m).
**Weights:** Empty 4,700lb (2134kg); loaded 7,510lb (3410kg).
**Performance:** Maximum speed 138mph (222km/h); initial climb 1,220ft (372m)/min; service ceiling 19,250ft (5867m); range with full ordnance load 546 miles (879km).
**Armament:** One fixed 0·303in Vickers, one manually aimed 0·303in Browning or Vickers K in rear cockpit; crutch for 18in 1,610lb torpedo (or 1,500lb mine or 1,500lb of bombs). (Mk II-IV) underwing racks for eight 60lb rockets or other stores.
**History:** First flight (TSR.II) 17 April 1934; production Mk I December 1935; service delivery February 1936; final delivery June 1944.
**User:** UK (RN).

**Development:** One of the great combat aircraft of history, the well-loved "Stringbag" looked archaic even when new, yet outlasted the aircraft intended to replace it and served valiantly and successfully from countless carriers and rough airstrips from start to finish of World War II. Designed to Specification S.38/34, it derived from an earlier prototype which got into an uncontrollable spin. Designated TSR.II the revised aircraft had a longer, spin-proof body, necessitating sweeping back the upper wing slightly. All-metal, with fabric covering, pre-war Swordfish were often twin-float seaplanes, these usually serving in the three-seat spotter role. Most, however, equipped the Fleet Air Arm's 13 landplane torpedo squadrons and during World War II a further 13 were formed. Stories of this amazingly willing aircraft are legion. One aircraft made twelve minelaying sorties in 24 hours. Another torpedoed an enemy ship in a round trip taking ten hours. A handful based in Malta sank an average of 50,000 tons of enemy vessels (most very heavily armed with flak) every month in 1941-43. The highlight of the Swordfish's career was the attack on the Italian naval base of Taranto, on 10–11 November 1940, when two Swordfish were lost in exchange for the destruction of three battleships, a cruiser, two destroyers and other warships. The Mk II had metal-skinned lower wings for rocket-firing, the III had radar and the IV an enclosed cockpit. From 1940 all production and development was handled by Blackburn, which built 1,699 of the 2,391 delivered.

**Right: One of the landplane Swordfish from the second production batch in 1935, pictured in wartime naval camouflage.**

**Below: No combat aircraft of World War II left a greater legacy of willing work. These paint-flaking Mk IIs, built by Blackburn, were on duty in 1944.**

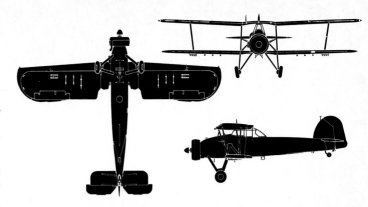

**Above: Swordfish IV, the final mark with an enclosed cockpit.**

**Below: Probably taken in early 1942, this scene shows "Stringbags" huddled on the constricted deck of an escort carrier.**

# General Aircraft Hamilcar

## G.A.L.49 Hamilcar and G.A.L.58 Hamilcar X

**Origin:** General Aircraft Ltd, Hanworth; production assigned to Birmingham Railway Carriage & Wagon Co, assisted by Co-operative Wholesale Society and AC Cars Ltd.
**Type:** Heavy assault glider.
**Engines:** None; (Mk X) two 965hp Bristol Mercury 31 nine-cylinder radial.
**Dimensions:** Span 110ft 0in (33·53m); length 68ft 0in (20·73m); height 20ft 3in (6·17m).
**Weights:** Empty 18,400lb (8346kg), (X) 25,510lb (11,571kg); maximum 36,000lb (16,330kg) (some, 37,000lb), (X) 47,000lb (21,319kg).
**Performance:** Tow limit speed 150mph (241km/h); maximum speed (glider in dive) 187mph (301km/h), (X) 145mph (232km/h); stalling speed 65mph (105km/h).
**History:** First flight 27 March 1942; service delivery early 1943; first flight (Mk X) February 1945.
**User:** UK (RAF).

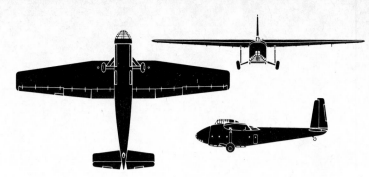

**Above: Three-view of Hamilcar with practice landing gear.**

**Right: Flight near Dishforth, Yorkshire, of the prototype Hamilcar (with gear jettisoned) in 1942, towed by a Halifax II.**

**Development:** Designed to Specification X.27/40, the Hamilcar was the largest Allied glider to see action. It was planned to carry the vehicles and weapons that could not previously accompany airborne troops, typical loads being a 17-pounder gun and tug, the specially designed Tetrarch and Locust tanks, two Universal Carriers, or a wide range of scrapers, dozers and Bailey bridge gear. Built of wood, the Hamilcar was awesomely big. The two pilots climbed up the right side of the cavernous interior, emerged through a roof hatch 15ft (4·6m) above the ground and walked along a sloping and possibly icy roof to their tandem cockpits. Halifax and Stirling tugs pulled over 70 to Normandy in the small hours of D-day, and many more were used in the Market Garden and Rhine-crossing operations. Altogether GAL built 22 and the BRC&W group 390, with another 290 cancelled in early 1945. The Mk X, intended for the Far East, could operate as a conventional aircraft with 3½-ton load, and fly out of its destination field, or carry the full 9-ton load with a tug. Without payload the Mk X, of which only 22 were built by VJ-day, could fly 1,675 miles (2695km).

# Gloster Gladiator

## S.S.37 Gladiator I and II and Sea Gladiator

**Origin:** Gloster Aircraft Company.
**Type:** Single-seat fighter; (Sea Gladiator) carrier-based fighter.
**Engine:** One 840hp Bristol Mercury IX or IXS nine-cylinder radial; (Gladiator II) usually Mercury VIIIA of similar power.
**Dimensions:** Span 32ft 3in (9·85m); length 27ft 5in (8·38m); height 10ft 4in (3·17m).
**Weights:** Empty 3,450lb (1565kg); (Sea Gladiator) 3,745lb; loaded 4,750lb (2155kg); (Sea Gladiator) 5,420lb.
**Performance:** Maximum speed 253mph (407km/h); (Sea Gladiator) 245mph; initial climb 2,300ft (700m)/min; service ceiling 33,000ft (10,060m); range 440 miles (708km); (Sea Gladiator) 425 miles.
**Armament:** First 71 aircraft, two 0·303in Vickers in fuselage, one 0·303in Lewis under each lower wing; subsequent, four 0·303in Brownings in same locations, fuselage guns with 600 rounds and wing guns with 400.
**History:** First flight (S.S.37) September 1934; (Gladiator I) June 1936; (Sea Gladiator) 1938; service delivery March 1937; final delivery April 1940.
**Users:** Belgium, China, Egypt, Finland, Greece, Iraq, Ireland, Latvia, Lithuania, Norway, Portugal, South Africa, Sweden, UK (RAF, RN).

**Development:** Air Ministry Specification F.7/30 recognised that future fighters would have to be faster and better armed, but the delay in placing an order extended to a disgraceful 4½ years, by which time war clouds were distantly gathering and the fabric-covered biplane was swiftly to be judged obsolete. Folland's S.S.37 was built as a very late entrant, long after the competition to F.7/30 ought to have been settled. Though less radical than most contenders it was eventually judged best and, as the Gladiator, was at last ordered in July 1935. Features included neat single-bay wings, each of the four planes having small hydraulically depressed drag flaps; cantilever landing gear with Dowty internally sprung wheels; four guns; and, in the production aircraft, a sliding cockpit canopy. Most early production had the Watts wooden propeller, though performance was better with the three-blade metal Fairey-Reed type. The Mk II aircraft introduced desert filters, auto mixture control and electric starter from internal battery. The Sea Gladiator had full carrier equipment and a dinghy. Total production amounted to at least 767, including 480 for the RAF, 60 Sea Gladiators and

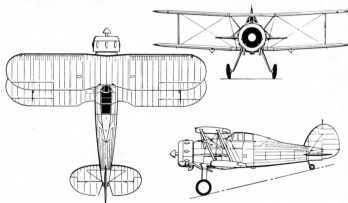

**Above: Three-view of Gladiator I (II similar).**

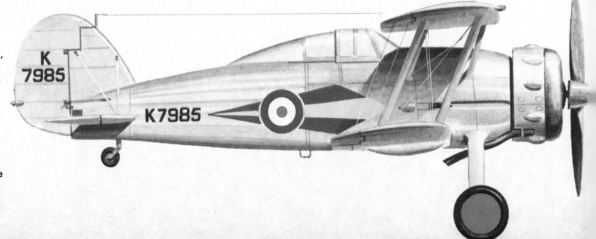

**Right: This Gladiator I, seen in the markings of 73 Sqn in 1938, was one of the second production batch, in 1937. In the course of this batch the newly licensed Browning machine gun became available, but the propeller remained the original wooden two-blade type until 1939.**

216 exported to 12 foreign countries. Gladiators of the Auxiliary Air Force intercepted the first bombing raid on Britain, over the Firth of Forth in September 1939, and these highly manoeuvrable biplanes were constantly in heroic action for the next three years. Aircraft from the torpedoed *Glorious* operated from a frozen lake in Norway and three Sea Gladiators defended Malta against the Regia Aeronautica from 11 June 1940.

**Left:** In 1937-40 the Gladiator was Britain's most exported aircraft and the small Gloster staff had to scheme numerous foreign armament and equipment fits. This example is one of a batch of 26 bought by Latvia, a country which relied on Britain for most of its military aircraft.

**Below:** The spirit of the RAF in the first months of war is captured exquisitely in this photograph of one of the then-new fighters beating up a car on the grass airfield (probably the CO's, because special-bodied coupés were not for junior pilots on a few shillings a day). This machine has the Fairey three-blade metal propeller later made standard.

**Below:** The Gladiator was the only effective fighter of the Norwegian Army Flying Service when the Luftwaffe invaded in April 1940. This ski-equipped example served with the Jager-avdeling (fighter flight) at Oslo-Fornebu. It took on Bf 110s.

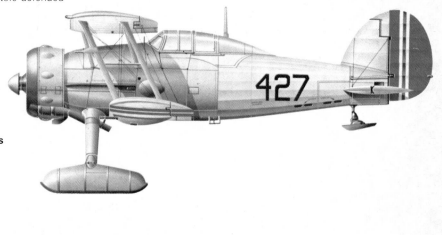

# Gloster G-41 Meteor

## G.41 Meteor I and II

**Origin:** Gloster Aircraft Company; (post-war, other builders).
**Type:** Single-seat fighter.
**Engines:** Two Rolls-Royce centrifugal turbojets (sub-types, see text).
**Dimensions:** Span 43ft 0in (13·1m); length 41ft 4in (12·6m); height 13ft 0in (3·96m).
**Weights:** Empty 8,140lb (3693kg); loaded 13,800lb (6260kg).
**Performance:** Maximum speed (I) 410mph (660km/h); initial climb (I) 2,155ft (657m)/min; service ceiling 40,000–44,000ft (12,192–13,410m); range on internal fuel about 1,000 miles at altitude (1610km).
**Armament:** Four 20mm Hispano cannon on sides of nose.
**History:** First flight (prototype) 5 March 1943; squadron delivery (F.I) 12 July 1944.
**Users:** UK (RAF), US (AAF, one, on exchange); (post-war, many air forces).

**Development:** Designed to Specification F.9/40 by George Carter, the Gloster G.41 was to have been named Thunderbolt, but when this name was given to the P-47 the Gloster twin-jet became the Meteor. The first Allied jet combat design, it was surprisingly large, with generous wing area. Though this made the early marks poor performers even on two engines, it proved beneficial in the long term, because marvellous engine development by Rolls-Royce transformed the Meteor into a multi-role aircraft with outstanding speed, acceleration and climb and, thanks to its ample proportions, it could be developed for such challenging roles as advanced dual training,

**Above: The sliding canopy identifies this as a Meteor III, first major production version of the first Allied combat jet. After the first 15 Meteror IIIs had been completed with Welland engines, the 2,000lb Rolls-Royce Derwent was installed the remainder of more than 200 built. By early 1945 the Meteor III was in service with the 2nd Tactical Air Force, and the first operational sortie was flown in April.**

**Gloster Meteor F.III cutaway drawing key**

1 Starboard detachable wingtip
2 Starboard navigation light
3 Starboard recognition light
4 Starboard aileron
5 Aileron balance tab
6 Aileron mass balance weights
7 Aileron control coupling
8 Aileron torque shaft
9 Chain sprocket
10 Cross-over control runs
11 Front spar
12 Rear spar
13 Aileron (inboard) mass balance
14 Nacelle detachable tail section
15 Jet pipe exhaust
16 Internal stabilising struts
17 Rear spar 'spectacle' frame
18 Fire extinguisher spray ring
19 Main engine mounting frame
20 Engine access panel(s)
21 Nacelle nose structure
22 Intake internal leading-edge shroud
23 Starboard engine intake
24 Windscreen de-icing spray tube
25 Reflector gunsight
26 Cellular glass bullet-proof windscreen
27 Aft-sliding cockpit canopy
28 Demolition incendiary (cockpit starboard wall)
29 RPM indicators (left and right of gunsight)
30 Pilot's seat
31 Forward fuselage top deflector skin
32 Gun wobble button
33 Control column grip
34 Main instrument panel
35 Nosewheel armoured bulkhead
36 Nose release catches (10)
37 Nosewheel jack bulkhead housing/attachment
38 Nose ballast weight location
39 Nosewheel mounting frames
40 Radius rod (link and jack omitted)
41 Nosewheel pivot bearings
42 Shimmy-damper/self-centring strut
43 Gun camera
44 Camera access
45 Aperture
46 Nose cone
47 Cabin cold-air intake
48 Nosewheel leg door

49 Picketing rings
50 Tension shock absorber
51 Pivot bracket
52 Mudguard
53 Torque strut
54 Door hoop
55 Wheel fork
56 Retractable nosewheel
57 Nosewheel doors
58 Port cannon trough fairings
59 Nosewheel cover
60 Intermediate diaphragm
61 Blast tubes
62 Gun front mounting rails
63 Pilot's seat pan
64 Emergency crowbar
65 Canopy de-misting silica gel cylinder
66 Bullet-proof glass rear-view cut-outs
67 Canopy track
68 Seat bulkhead
69 Entry step
70 Link ejection chutes
71 Case ejection chutes
72 20-mm Hispano Mk III cannon
73 Belt feed mechanism
74 Ammunition feed necks
75 Ammunition tanks
76 Aft glazing (magazine bay top door)
77 Loading ramp
78 Front spar bulkhead
79 Oxygen bottles (2)
80 Front spar carry-through

81 Tank bearer frames
82 Rear spar carry-through
83 Self-sealing (twin compartment) main fuel tank, capacity 165 Imp gal (750 l) in each half
84 Fuel connector pipe
85 Return pipe
86 Drain pipes
87 Fuel filler caps
88 Tank doors (2)
89 T.R. 1143 aerial mast
90 Rear spar bulkhead (plywood face)
91 Aerial support frame
92 R.3121 (or B.C.966A) IFF installation
93 Tab control cables

94 Amplifier
95 Fire extinguisher bottles (2)
96 Elevator torque shaft
97 T.R.1143 transmitter/receiver radio installation
98 Pneumatic system filter

99 Pneumatic system (compressed) air cylinders
100 Tab cable fairlead
101 Elevator control cable
102 Top longeron
103 Fuselage frame
104 IFF aerial
105 DR compass master unit
106 Rudder cables
107 Starboard lower longeron
108 Cable access panels (port and starboard)
109 Tail section joint
110 Rudder linkage

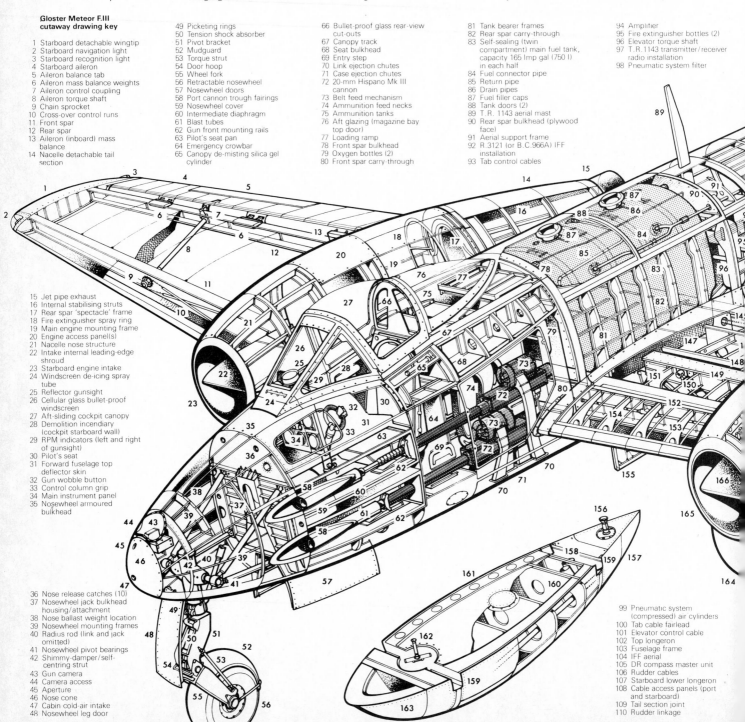

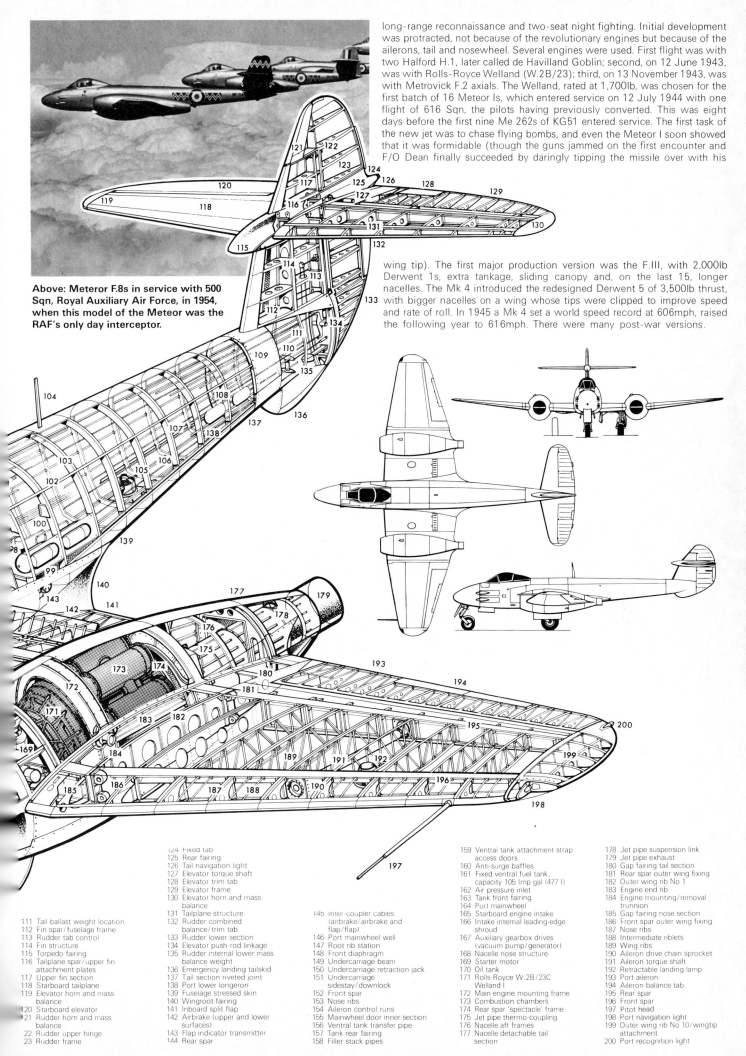

long-range reconnaissance and two-seat night fighting. Initial development was protracted, not because of the revolutionary engines but because of the ailerons, tail and nosewheel. Several engines were used. First flight was with two Halford H.1, later called de Havilland Goblin; second, on 12 June 1943, was with Rolls-Royce Welland (W.2B/23); third, on 13 November 1943, was with Metrovick F.2 axials. The Welland, rated at 1,700lb, was chosen for the first batch of 16 Meteor Is, which entered service on 12 July 1944 with one flight of 616 Sqn, the pilots having previously converted. This was eight days before the first nine Me 262s of KG51 entered service. The first task of the new jet was to chase flying bombs, and even the Meteor I soon showed that it was formidable (though the guns jammed on the first encounter and F/O Dean finally succeeded by daringly tipping the missile over with his

**Above: Meteor F.8s in service with 500 Sqn, Royal Auxiliary Air Force, in 1954, when this model of the Meteor was the RAF's only day interceptor.**

wing tip). The first major production version was the F.III, with 2,000lb Derwent 1s, extra tankage, sliding canopy and, on the last 15, longer nacelles. The Mk 4 introduced the redesigned Derwent 5 of 3,500lb thrust, with bigger nacelles on a wing whose tips were clipped to improve speed and rate of roll. In 1945 a Mk 4 set a world speed record at 606mph, raised the following year to 616mph. There were many post-war versions.

111 Tail ballast weight location
112 Fin spar/fuselage frame
113 Rudder tab control
114 Fin structure
115 Torpedo fairing
116 Tailplane spar/upper fin attachment plates
117 Upper fin section
118 Starboard tailplane
119 Elevator horn and mass balance
120 Starboard elevator
121 Rudder horn and mass balance
122 Rudder upper hinge
123 Rudder frame
124 Fixed tab
125 Rear fairing
126 Tail navigation light
127 Elevator torque shaft
128 Elevator trim tab
129 Elevator frame
130 Elevator horn and mass balance
131 Tailplane structure
132 Rudder combined balance/trim tab
133 Rudder lower section
134 Elevator push-rod linkage
135 Rudder internal lower mass balance weight
136 Emergency landing tailskid
137 Tail section riveted joint
138 Port lower longeron
139 Fuselage stressed skin
140 Wingroot fairing
141 Inboard split flap
142 Airbrake (upper and lower surfaces)
143 Flap indicator transmitter
144 Rear spar
145 Inter-coupler cables (airbrake/airbrake and flap/flap)
146 Port mainwheel well
147 Root rib station
148 Front diaphragm
149 Undercarriage beam
150 Undercarriage retraction jack
151 Undercarriage sidestay/downlock
152 Front spar
153 Nose ribs
154 Aileron control runs
155 Mainwheel door inner section
156 Ventral tank transfer pipe
157 Tank rear fairing
158 Filler stack pipes
159 Ventral tank attachment strap access doors
160 Anti-surge baffles
161 Fixed ventral fuel tank, capacity 105 Imp gal (477 l)
162 Air pressure inlet
163 Tank front fairing
164 Port mainwheel
165 Starboard engine intake
166 Intake internal leading-edge shroud
167 Auxiliary gearbox drives (vacuum pump/generator)
168 Nacelle nose structure
169 Starter motor
170 Oil tank
171 Rolls-Royce W.2B/23C Welland I
172 Main engine mounting frame
173 Combustion chambers
174 Rear spar 'spectacle' frame
175 Jet pipe thermo-coupling
176 Nacelle aft frames
177 Nacelle detachable tail section
178 Jet pipe suspension link
179 Jet pipe exhaust
180 Gap fairing tail section
181 Rear spar outer wing fixing
182 Outer wing rib No 1
183 Engine end rib
184 Engine mounting/removal trunnion
185 Gap fairing nose section
186 Front spar outer wing fixing
187 Nose ribs
188 Intermediate riblets
189 Wing ribs
190 Aileron drive chain sprocket
191 Aileron torque shaft
192 Retractable landing lamp
193 Port aileron
194 Aileron balance tab
195 Rear spar
196 Front spar
197 Pitot head
198 Port navigation light
199 Outer wing rib No 10/wingtip attachment
200 Port recognition light

# Handley Page Hampden

## H.P.52 Hampden I and H.P.53 Hereford I

**Origin:** Handley Page Ltd; also built by English Electric Co. and Canadian Associated Aircraft.

**Type:** Four-seat bomber (Hampden, later torpedo bomber and minelayer).

**Engines:** (Hampden) two 1,000hp Bristol Pegasus XVIII nine-cylinder radials; (Hereford) two 1,000hp Napier Dagger VIII 24-cylinder H-type air-cooled.

**Dimensions:** Span 69ft 2in (21·98m); length 53ft 7in (16·33m); height 14ft 4in (4·37m).

**Weights:** Empty (Hampden) 11,780lb (5344kg); (Hereford) 11,700lb (5308kg); loaded (Hampden) 18,756lb (8508kg); (Hereford) 16,000lb (7257kg).

**Performance:** (Hampden) maximum speed 254mph (410km/h); initial climb 980ft (300m)/min; service ceiling 19,000ft (5790m); range with maximum bomb load 1,095 miles (1762km).

**Armament:** Originally, one offensive 0·303in Vickers fixed firing ahead, one 0·303in Lewis manually aimed from nose by nav/bomb aimer, one Lewis manually aimed by wireless operator from upper rear position and one Lewis manually aimed by lower rear gunner; bomb load of 4,000lb (1814kg). By January 1940 both rear positions had twin 0·303in Vickers K with increased field of fire. Hard points for two 500lb bombs added below outer wings, provision for carrying mines or one 18in torpedo internally.

**History:** First flight (H.P.52 prototype) 21 June 1936; (production Hampden I) May 1938; (Hereford I) December 1939; termination of production March 1942.

**Users:** Canada, New Zealand, UK (RAF).

**Development:** On paper the Hampden, the last of the monoplane bombers to enter RAF service during the Expansion Scheme of 1936—38, was a truly outstanding aircraft. The makers considered it so fast and manoeuvrable they called it "a fighting bomber" and gave the pilot a fixed gun. They judged the three movable guns gave complete all-round defence without the penalties of heavy turrets and, while the Hampden was almost the equal of the big Whitley and Wellington in range with heavy bomb load, it was much faster than either; it was almost as fast as the Blenheim, but carried four times the load twice as far (on only fractionally greater power). Thanks to its well flapped and slatted wing it could land as slowly as 73mph. Designed to B.9/32, the prototype was angular but the production machine, to 30/36. looked very attractive and large orders were placed, eight squadrons being operational in September 1939 raiding German naval installations and ships (bombing German land was forbidden), until the daylight formations encountered enemy fighters. Then casualties were so heavy the Hampden was taken off operations and re-equipped with much better armament and armour — and, more to the point, used only at night. Despite cramp and near-impossibility of getting from one crew position to another, the "Flying Suitcase" had a successful career bombing invasion barges in the summer of 1940, bombing German heartlands, mine-laying and, finally, as a long-range torpedo bomber over the North Sea and northern Russia. Handley Page built 500, English Electric built 770 and Canadian Associated Aircraft 160. Short Brothers built 100 Herefords which never became operational; many were converted to Hampdens.

**Below:** A formation of 44 Sqn Hampden Is. Large numbers of this promising bomber were ordered from 1936, and eight squadrons were equipped with the type at the start of the war, but daylight operations were halted by the end of 1939.

Above: A Hampden I of 455 Sqn, Leuchars. The Hampden was perhaps the RAF bomber that most closely followed the philosophy of Luftwaffe bombers and yet, unlike the British aircraft, the Do17Z, He 111 and Ju88 had to continue on the thick of battle through lack of a replacement.

Above: A Hampden of 44 (Rhodesia) Sqn at Waddington, which in 1941-42 became the first unit to convert to the Lancaster. By this time the new roundels had narrow white and yellow rings.

Left: Dorsal gunner's view of squadron playmates, probably in 1939. The Hampden was outstandingly manoeuvrable, but was found to be a death-trap in daylight against Bf 109s.

Below: Hampden I in 1940 with twin dorsal and ventral guns.

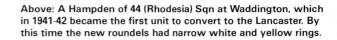

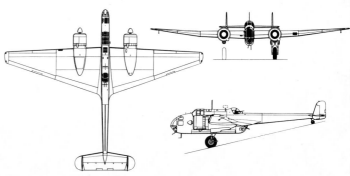

# Handley Page Halifax

## H.P.57 Halifax I, H.P.59 Mk II Series 1A, III, H.P.61 Mk V, B.VI and VII, C.VIII and A.IX

**Origin:** Handley Page Ltd; also built by London Aircraft Production Group, English Electric Ltd, Rootes Securities (Speke) and Fairey Aviation Ltd (Stockport).

**Type:** Seven-seat heavy bomber; later ECM platform, special transport and glider tug, cargo transport and paratroop carrier.

**Engines:** Four Rolls-Royce Merlin vee-12 liquid-cooled or Bristol Hercules 14-cylinder two-row sleeve-valve radial (see text).

**Dimensions:** Span (I to early III) 98ft 10in (30·12m); (from later III) 104ft 2in (31·75m); length (I, II, III Srs 1) 70ft 1in (21·36m); (II Srs 1A onwards) 71ft 7in (21·82m); height 20ft 9in (6·32m).

**Weights:** Empty (I Srs 1) 33,860lb (15,359kg); (II Srs 1A) 35,270lb (16,000kg); (VI) 39,000lb (17,690kg); loaded (I) 55,000lb (24,948kg); (I Srs 1) 58,000lb (26,308kg); (I Srs 2) 60,000lb (27,216kg); (II) 60,000lb; (II Srs 1A) 63,000lb (28,576kg), (III) 65,000lb (29,484kg), (V) 60,000lb; (VI) 68,000lb (30,844kg); (VII, VIII, IX) 65,000lb.

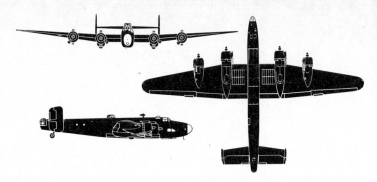

**Above: Three-view of the extended-span Halifax B.III Series II (Mk VI similar). Most had $H_2S$ radar fitted.**

**Left: A Halifax B.III Series II with extended wings and $H_2S$, serving with 640 Sqn at Leconfield, Yorkshire. Vivid tails were common among the multi-national Halifax units.**

**Below: An early Halifax II Series I with Boulton-Paul two-gun dorsal turret, on factory test.**

Above: **L9530 was one of the first production batch in 1940. Serving with 76 Sqn (MP-L) it had manual beam guns and prominent fuel-jettison pipes passing beneath the flaps. The photograph must have been taken from the right beam gun position of an accompanying Halifax, in mid-1941.**

**Performance:** Maximum speed (I) 265mph (426km/h); (II) 270mph (435km/h); (III, VI) 312mph (501km/h); (V, VII, VIII, IX) 285mph (460 km/h); initial climb (typical) 750ft (229m)/min; service ceiling, typically (Merlin) 22,800ft (6950m); (Hercules) 24,000ft (7315m); range with maximum load (I) 980 miles (1577km); (II) 1,100 miles (1770km); (III, VI) 1,260 miles (2030km).

**Armament:** See text.

**History:** First flight (prototype) 25 October 1939; (production Mk I) 11 October 1940; squadron delivery 23 November 1940; first flight (production III) July 1943; final delivery 20 November 1946.

**Users:** Australia, Canada, France (FFL), New Zealand, UK (RAF, BOAC).

**Development:** Though it never attained the limelight and glamour of its partner, the Lancaster, the "Halibag" made almost as great a contribution to Allied victory in World War II, and it did so in a far greater diversity of roles. Planned as a twin-Vulture bomber to Specification P.13/36 with a gross weight of 26,300lb it grew to weigh 68,000lb as a formidable weapon platform and transport that suffered from no vices once it had progressed through a succession of early changes. By far the biggest change, in the summer of 1937, was to switch from two Vultures to four Merlins (a godsend, as it turned out) and the first 100 H.P.57s were ordered on 3 September 1937. This version, the Mk I, had a 22ft bomb bay and six bomb cells in the wing centre-section. Engines were 1,280hp Merlin X and defensive armament comprised two 0·303in Brownings in the nose turret, four in the tail turret and, usually, two in manual beam positions. The first squadron was No 35 at Linton on Ouse and the first mission Le Havre on the night of 11/12 March 1942. The I Srs 2 was stressed to 60,000lb and the Srs 3 had more fuel. The Mk II had 1,390hp Merlin XX and Hudson-type twin-0·303in dorsal turret instead of beam guns. On the II Srs 1 Special the front and dorsal turrets and engine flame dampers were all removed to improve performance. The II Srs 1A introduced what became the standard nose, a clear Perspex moulding with manually aimed 0·303in Vickers K, as well as the Defiant-type 4×0·303in dorsal turret and 1,390hp Merlin XXII. Later Srs 1A introduced larger fins which improved bombing accuracy; one of these, with radome under the rear fuselage, was the first aircraft to use H$_2$S ground-mapping radar on active service. In November 1942 the GR.II Srs 1A entered service with Coastal Command, with 0·5in nose gun, marine equipment and often four-blade propellers. The III overcame all the performance problems with 1,650hp Hercules and DH Hydromatic propellers, later IIIs having the wings extended to rounded tips giving better field length, climb, ceiling and range. The IV (turbocharged Hercules) was not built. The V was a II Srs 2A with Dowty landing gear and hydraulics (Messier on other marks), used as a bomber, Coastal GR, ASW and meteorological aircraft. The VI was the definitive bomber, with 1,800hp Hercules 100 and extra tankage and full tropical equipment. The VII was a VI using old Hercules XVI. The C.VIII was an unarmed transport with large quick-change 8,000lb cargo pannier in place of the bomb bay and 11 passenger seats; it led to the post-war Halton civil transport. The A.IX carried 16 paratroops and associated cargo. The III, V, VII and IX served throughout Europe towing gliders and in other special operations, including airdropping agents and arms to Resistance groups and carrying electronic countermeasures (ECM) with 100 Group. Total production amounted to 6,176, by H.P., English Electric, the London Aircraft Production Group (London Transport), Fairey and Rootes, at a peak rate of one per hour. Final mission was by a GR.VI from Gibraltar in March 1952, the Armée de l'Air phasing out its B.VI at about the same time.

# Hawker Hurricane

## Hurricane I to XII, Sea Hurricane IA to XIIA

**Origin:** Hawker Aircraft Ltd; also built by Gloster Aircraft, SABCA (Belgium) and Canadian Car & Foundry Inc.

**Type:** Single-seat fighter; later, fighter-bomber, tank buster and ship-based fighter.

**Engine:** One Rolls-Royce Merlin vee-12 liquid-cooled (see text for sub-types).

**Dimensions:** Span 40ft (12·19m); length 32ft (9·75m); (Mk I) 31ft 5in; (Sea Hurricanes) 32ft 3in; height 13ft 1in (4m).

**Weights:** Empty (I) 4,670lb (2118kg); (IIA) 5,150lb (2335kg); (IIC) 5,640lb (2558kg); (IID) 5,800lb (2631kg); (IV) 5,550lb (2515kg); (Sea H.IIC) 5,788lb (2625kg); loaded (I) 6,600lb (2994kg); (IIA) 8,050lb (3650kg); (IIC) 8,250lb (3742kg); (IID) 8,200lb (3719kg); (IV) 8,450lb (3832kg); (Sea H. IIC) 8,100lb (3674kg).

**Performance:** Maximum speed (I) 318mph (511km/h); (IIA, B, C) 345–335mph (560–540km/h); (IID) 286mph (460km/h); (IV) 330mph (531km/h); (Sea H. IIC) 342mph (550km/h); initial climb (I) 2,520ft (770m)/min; (IIA) 3,150ft (960m)/min; (rest, typical) 2,700ft (825m)/min; service ceiling (I) 36,000ft (10.973m); (IIA) 41,000ft (12,500m); (rest, typical) 34,000ft (10,365m); range (all, typical) 460 miles (740km), or with two 44 Imp gal drop tanks 950 miles (1530km).

**Armament:** (I) eight 0·303in Brownings, each with 333 rounds (Belgian model, four 0·5in FN-Brownings); (IIA) same, with provision for 12 guns and two 250lb bombs; (IIB) 12 Brownings and two 250 or 500lb bombs; (IIC) four 20mm Hispano cannon and bombs; (IID) two 40mm Vickers S guns and two 0·303in Brownings; (IV) universal wing with two Brownings and two Vickers S, two 500lb bombs, eight rockets, smoke installation or other stores.

**History:** First flight (prototype) 6 November 1935; (production Mk I) 12 October 1937; (II) 11 June 1940; (Canadian Mk X) January 1940; final delivery September 1944.

**Users:** (Wartime) Australia, Belgium, Canada, Czechoslovakia, Egypt, Finland, India, Iran, Iraq, Ireland, Jugoslavia, New Zealand, Poland, Portugal, Romania, South Africa, Soviet Union, Turkey, UK (RAF, RN).

▶

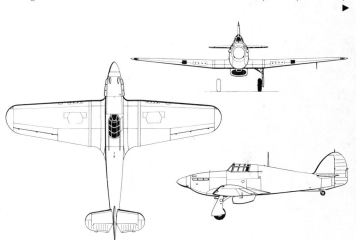

Above: **Three-view of Hurricane I (with metal-skinned wings).**

Below: **The Hawker High-Speed Monoplane (F.36/34) prototype, flown in November 1935 a few weeks after the first Bf 109. Many detail changes were needed to yield the Hurricane.**

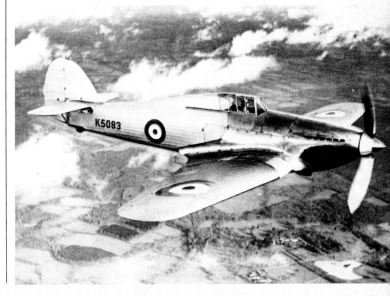

**► Development:** Until well into 1941 the Hurricane was by far the most numerous of the RAF's combat aircraft and it bore the brunt of the early combats with the Luftwaffe over France and Britain. Designed by Camm as a Fury Monoplane, with Goshawk engine and spatted landing gear, it was altered on the drawing board to have the more powerful PV.12 (Merlin) and inwards-retracting gear and, later, to have not four machine guns but the unprecedented total of eight. The Air Ministry wrote Specification F.36/34 around it and after tests with the prototype ordered the then-fantastic total of 600 in June 1936. In September 1939 the 497 delivered equipped 18 squadrons and by 7 August 1940 no fewer than 2,309 had been delivered, compared with 1,383 Spitfires, equipping 32 squadrons, compared with 18½ Spitfire squadrons. Gloster's output in 1940 was 130 per month. By this time the Hurricane I was in service with new metal-skinned wings, instead

**Above:** Seen in post-war markings, this Hurricane (Langley-built IIC BD867) shows the constant-speed propeller that became standard in 1941.

**Left:** Hurricane I of 2e Escadrille ''Le Chardon'', Regiment I/2 at Diest, 1940. The Belgian aircraft had armament of four 0·5in FN-Brownings.

**Hawker Hurricane Mk IIC cutaway drawing key:**

1 Starboard navigation light
2 Starboard wingtip
3 Aluminium alloy aileron
4 Self-aligning ball-bearing aileron hinge
5 Aft wing spar
6 Aluminium alloy wing skinning (early Hurricanes, fabric)
7 Forward wing spar
8 Starboard landing light
9 Rotol or DH three-blade constant-speed propeller
10 Spinner
11 Propeller hub
12 Pitch-control mechanism
13 Spinner back plate
14 Cowling fairings
15 Coolant pipes
16 Rolls-Royce Merlin XX 12-cylinder engine, 1,185 hp
17 Cowling panel fasteners
18 'Fishtail' exhaust pipes
19 Electric generator
20 Engine forward mounting feet
21 Engine upper bearer tube
22 Engine forward mount
23 Engine lower bearer tubes
24 Starboard mainwheel fairing
25 Starboard mainwheel
26 Low pressure tyre
27 Brake drum (pneumatic brakes)
28 Hand-cranked inertia starter
29 Hydraulic system
30 Bearer joint
31 Auxiliary intake
32 Carburettor air intake
33 Wing root fillet
34 Engine oil drain collector/ breather
35 Fuel pump drain
36 Engine aft bearers
37 Magneto
38 Two-stage supercharger
39 Cowling panel attachments
40 Engine tachometer
41 External bead sight
42 Removable aluminium alloy cowling panels
43 Engine coolant header tank
44 Engine firewall (armour-plated backing)
45 Fuselage (reserve) fuel tank (28 gal/127 litres)
46 Exhaust glare shield
47 Control column
48 Engine bearer attachment
49 Rudder pedals
50 Control linkage
51 Centre-section fuel tank (optional)
52 Oil system piping
53 Pneumatic system air cylinder
54 Wing centre-section/front spar girder construction
55 Engine bearer support strut
56 Oil tank (port wing root leading-edge)
57 Dowty undercarriage ram
58 Port undercarriage well
59 Wing centre-section girder frame
60 Pilot's oxygen cylinder
61 Elevator trim-tab control wheel
62 Radiator flap control lever
63 Entry footstep
64 Fuselage tubular framework
65 Landing lamp control lever
66 Oxygen supply cock

67 Throttle lever
68 Safety harness
69 Pilot's seat
70 Pilot's break-out exit panel
71 Map case
72 Instrument panel
73 Cockpit ventilation inlet
74 Reflector gunsight
75 Bullet-proof windscreen
76 Rear-view mirror
77 Rearward-sliding canopy
78 Canopy frames
79 Canopy handgrip
80 Perspex canopy panels
81 Head/back armour plate
82 Harness attachment
83 Aluminium alloy decking
84 Turnover reinforcement
85 Canopy track
86 Fuselage framework cross-bracing
87 Radio equipment (TR9D/TR133)
88 Support tray
89 Removable access panel
90 Aileron cable drum
91 Elevator control lever
92 Cable adjusters
93 Aluminium alloy wing/ fuselage fillet
94 Ventral identification and formation-keeping lights
95 Footstep retraction guide and support rail
96 Radio equipment (R3002)
97 Upward-firing recognition apparatus
98 Handhold
99 Diagonal support
100 Fuselage fairing
101 Dorsal identification light
102 Aerial mast
103 Aerial lead-in

104 Recognition apparatus cover panel
105 Mast support
106 Wire-braced upper truss
107 Wooden fuselage fairing formers
108 Fabric covering
109 Radio antenna
110 All-metal tailplane structure
111 Static and dynamic elevator balance
112 Starboard elevator
113 Light-alloy leading-edge
114 Fabric covering
115 Fin structure
116 Diagonal bracing struts
117 Built-in static balance
118 Aerial stub
119 Fabric-covered rudder
120 Rudder structure
121 Rudder post
122 Rear navigation light
123 Balanced rudder trim tab
124 Wiring
125 Elevator trim tab
126 Fixed balance tab

127 Fabric-covered elevator
128 Tailplane rear spar
129 Tailplane front spar
130 Rudder lower hinge
131 Rudder operating lever
132 Connecting rod
133 Control pulleys
134 Elevator operating lever
135 Tailplane spar attachments
136 Aluminium alloy tailplane/ fuselage fairing
137 Tailwheel shock-strut
138 Angled frame rear structure
139 Sternpost
140 Ventral fin
141 Dowty oleo-pneumatic fixed self-centering tailwheel
142 Fin framework
143 Handling-bar socket
144 Fabric covering
145 Swaged tube and steel gusset fitting and through-bolts
146 Upper tube/longeron
147 Rudder cables

148 Wooden stringers
149 Elevator cables
150 Aluminium alloy formers
151 Diagonal brace wires
152 Lower tube/longeron
153 Aluminium alloy former bottom section
154 Retractable entry footstep
155 Wing root fillet
156 Flap rod universal joint
157 Aileron cables
158 Fuselage/wing rear spar girder attachment
159 Main wing fuel tank (port and starboard: 33 gal/ 150 litres each)
160 Ventral Glycol radiator and oil cooler
161 Front spar wing fixings
162 Cannon forward mounting bracket
163 Cannon fairing
164 Recoil spring
165 Cannon barrels
166 Undercarriage retraction jack

**Above:** The cutaway drawing shows the very important Hurricane IIC, with more powerful engine and four 20mm cannon, which was the standard production sub-type in 1941.

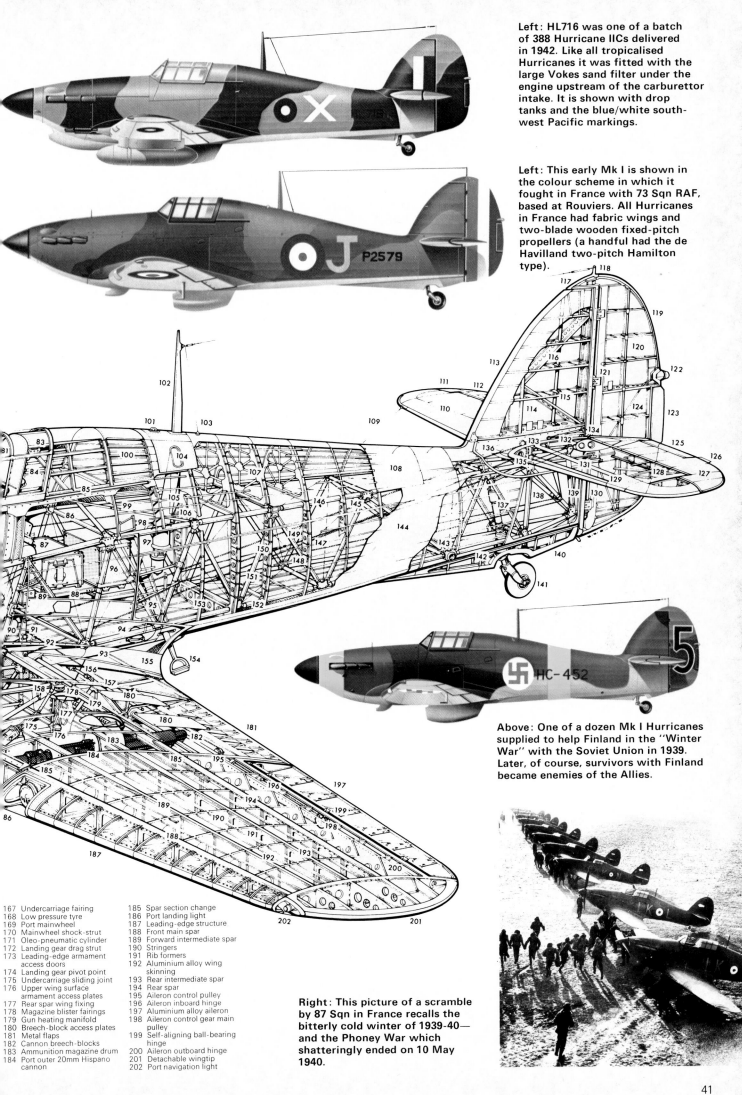

Left: HL716 was one of a batch of 388 Hurricane IICs delivered in 1942. Like all tropicalised Hurricanes it was fitted with the large Vokes sand filter under the engine upstream of the carburettor intake. It is shown with drop tanks and the blue/white south-west Pacific markings.

Left: This early Mk I is shown in the colour scheme in which it fought in France with 73 Sqn RAF, based at Rouviers. All Hurricanes in France had fabric wings and two-blade wooden fixed-pitch propellers (a handful had the de Havilland two-pitch Hamilton type).

Above: One of a dozen Mk I Hurricanes supplied to help Finland in the "Winter War" with the Soviet Union in 1939. Later, of course, survivors with Finland became enemies of the Allies.

167 Undercarriage fairing
168 Low pressure tyre
169 Port mainwheel
170 Mainwheel shock-strut
171 Oleo-pneumatic cylinder
172 Landing gear drag strut
173 Leading-edge armament access doors
174 Landing gear pivot point
175 Undercarriage sliding joint
176 Upper wing surface armament access plates
177 Rear spar wing fixing
178 Magazine blister fairings
179 Gun heating manifold
180 Breech-block access plates
181 Metal flaps
182 Cannon breech-blocks
183 Ammunition magazine drum
184 Port outer 20mm Hispano cannon

185 Spar section change
186 Port landing light
187 Leading-edge structure
188 Front main spar
189 Forward intermediate spar
190 Stringers
191 Rib formers
192 Aluminium alloy wing skinning
193 Rear intermediate spar
194 Rear spar
195 Aileron control pulley
196 Aileron inboard hinge
197 Aluminium alloy aileron
198 Aileron control gear main pulley
199 Self-aligning ball-bearing hinge
200 Aileron outboard hinge
201 Detachable wingtip
202 Port navigation light

Right: This picture of a scramble by 87 Sqn in France recalls the bitterly cold winter of 1939-40— and the Phoney War which shatteringly ended on 10 May 1940.

of fabric, and three-blade variable pitch (later constant-speed) propeller instead of the wooden Watts two-blader. In the hectic days of 1940 the Hurricane was found to be an ideal bomber destroyer, with steady sighting and devastating cone of fire; turn radius was better than that of any other monoplane fighter, but the all-round performance of the Bf 109E was considerably higher. The more powerful Mk II replaced the 1,030hp Merlin II by the 1,280hp Merlin XX and introduced new armament and drop tanks. In North West Europe it became a ground-attack aircraft, and in North Africa a tank-buster with 40mm guns. While operating from merchant-ship catapults and carriers it took part in countless fleet-defence actions, the greatest being the defence of the August 1942 Malta convoy, when 70 Sea Hurricanes fought off more than 600 Axis attackers, destroying 39 for the loss of seven fighters. The Hurricane was increasingly transferred to the Far East, Africa and other theatres, and 2,952 were dispatched to the Soviet Union, some receiving skis. Hurricanes were used for many special trials of armament and novel flight techniques (one having a jettisonable biplane upper wing). Total production amounted to 12,780 in Britain and 1,451 in Canada (after 1941 with Packard Merlins) and many hundreds were exported both before and after World War II.

**Right, upper:** A Hawker test pilot wringing out a production Mk I Hurricane in the neighbourhood of Brooklands shortly before the outbreak of World War II. The aircraft is one of 24 for Jugoslavia, which in April 1941 fought the Luftwaffe.

**Right, lower:** Like the Bf 110, Beaufighter and many other aircraft of World War II, the Hurricane was fairly soon outclassed as a daytime dogfighter, yet remained in production almost to the end of the conflict because it was versatile and useful. The last of all was PZ865, a Mk IIC bomber delivered in September 1944 bearing the inscription ''The Last of the Many'' (as distinct from ''The First of the Few'').

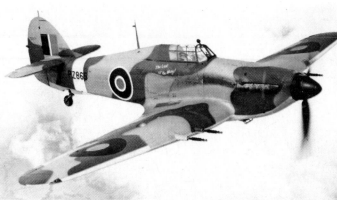

**Below:** Idyllic study of a Hurricane I (one of a batch of 600 built by Gloster) in formation with two Spitfires from a batch of 1,000 Mk IIAs and IIBs built at Castle Bromwich. The photograph was taken in 1942 when hundreds of these former front-line machines were standard equipment at OTUs (Operational Training Units), advanced flying training schools and such mundane establishments as Ferry Pilot Pools and Maintenance Units. It was common to cruise with the hood open when there was little likelihood of meeting the enemy.

# Hawker Typhoon

## Typhoon IA and IB

**Origin:** Hawker Aircraft Ltd; built by Gloster Aircraft Company.
**Type:** Single-seat fighter bomber.
**Engine:** (Production IB) one 2,180hp Napier Sabre II, 24-cylinder flat-H sleeve-valve liquid-cooled.
**Dimensions:** Span 41ft 7in (12·67m); length 31ft 11in (9·73m); height 15ft 3½in (4·66m).
**Weights:** Empty 8,800lb (3992kg); loaded 13,250lb (6010kg).
**Performance:** Maximum speed 412mph (664km/h); initial climb 3,000ft (914m)/min; service ceiling 35,200ft (10,730m); range (with bombs) 510 miles (821km), (with drop tanks) 980 miles (1577km).
**Armament:** (IA) 12 0·303in Brownings (none delivered); (IB) four 20mm Hispano cannon in outer wings, and racks for eight rockets or two 500lb (227kg) (later 1,000lb, 454kg) bombs.
**History:** First flight (Tornado) October 1939; (Typhoon) 24 February 1940; (production Typhoon) 27 May 1941; final delivery November 1945.
**Users:** Canada, New Zealand, UK (RAF).

**Development:** The Typhoon's early life was almost total disaster. Though the concept of so big and powerful a combat aircraft was bold and significant, expressed in Specification F.18/37, the Griffon and Centaurus engines were ignored and reliance was placed on the complex and untried Vulture and Sabre. The former powered the R-type fighter, later named Tornado, which ground to a halt with abandonment of the Vulture in early 1941. The N-type (Napier), named Typhoon, was held back six months by the desperate need for Hurricanes. Eventually, after most painful development, production began at Gloster Aircraft in 1941 and Nos 56 and 609 Sqns at Duxford began to re-equip with the big bluff-looking machine in September of that year. But the Sabre was unreliable, rate of climb and performance at height were disappointing and the rear fuselage persisted in coming apart. There was much talk of scrapping the programme, but, fortunately for the Allies, the snags were gradually overcome. In November 1942 the Typhoon suddenly sprang to favour by demonstrating it could catch and destroy the fastest fighter-bombers in the Luftwaffe which were making low-level hit-and-run raids. In 1943 "Tiffy" squadrons shot-up and blasted everything that moved in northern France and the Low Countries, and in the summer of 1944 the hundreds of Typhoons — by now thoroughly proven and capable of round-the-clock operation from rough forward strips — formed the backbone of 2nd Tactical Air Force attack strength, sending millions of cannon shells, rockets and heavy bombs into German ground forces and in a single day knocking out 175 tanks in the Falaise gap. Gloster built 3,315 of the 3,330 Typhoons, the final 3,000-odd having a clear bubble hood instead of a heavy-framed cockpit with a car-type door on each side.

**Above:** One of the main run of Mk IB Typhoons with the neat and unobstructed sliding teardrop hood. User is 54 Sqn.

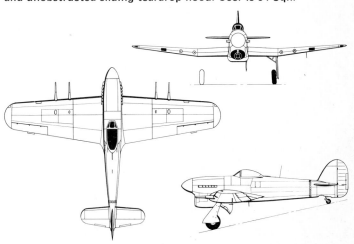

**Above:** Typhoon IB with sliding teardrop hood and whip aerial.

**Left:** A bombed-up Typhoon IB of 198 Sqn operating from Martragny, France, in July 1944.

**Below:** 175 Sqn servicing crew and an armourer with two 500-pounders tend one of the earlier Mk IB Typhoons with car-type doors and a rigid radio mast.

# Hawker Tempest

## Tempest V and VI

**Origin:** Hawker Aircraft Ltd; Mk II, Bristol Aeroplane Company.
**Type:** Single-seat fighter bomber.
**Engine:** (V) one 2,180hp Napier Sabre II 24-cylinder flat-H sleeve-valve liquid-cooled; (VI) one 2,340hp Sabre V.
**Dimensions:** Span 41ft (12·5m); length 33ft 8in (10·26m); height 16ft 1in (4·9m).
**Weights:** Empty 9,100lb (4128kg); loaded 13,500lb (6130kg).
**Performance:** Maximum speed (V) 427mph (688km/h); (VI) 438mph (704km/h); initial climb 3,000ft (914m)/min; service ceiling, about 37,000ft (11,280m); range (bombs, not tanks) 740 miles (1191km).
**Armament:** Four 20mm Hispano cannon in outer wings; underwing racks for eight rockets or up to 2,000lb (907kg) bombs.
**History:** First flight (prototype Mk V) 2 September 1942; (Mk I) 24 February 1943; (production V) 21 June 1943; (Mk II) 28 June 1943; (prototype VI) 9 May 1944; (production II) 4 October 1944.
**Users:** New Zealand, UK (RAF).

**Development:** The Typhoon was noted for its thick wing — occasional erratic flight behaviour at high speeds was traced to compressibility (local airflow exceeding the speed of sound), which had never before been encountered. In 1940 Hawker schemed a new laminar-flow wing with a root thickness five inches less and an elliptic planform rather like a Spitfire. This was used on the Typhoon II, ordered in November 1941 to Specification F.10/41, but there were so many changes the fighter was renamed Tempest. Fuel had to be moved from the thinner wing to the fuselage, making the latter longer, and a dorsal fin was added. The short-barrel Mk V guns were buried in the wing. Though the new airframe could take the promising Centaurus engine it was the Sabre-engined Mk V that was produced first, reaching the Newchurch Wing in time to destroy 638 out of the RAF's total of 1,771 flying bombs shot down in the summer of 1944. After building 800 Mk Vs Hawker turned out 142 of the more powerful Mk VI type with bigger radiator and oil coolers in the leading edge. After much delay, with production assigned first to Gloster and then to Bristol, the Centaurus-powered Mk II — much quieter and nicer to fly — entered service in November 1945, and thus missed the war. A few Mks 5 and 6 (post-war designations) were converted as target tugs.

**Below:** This Tempest was built as a Mk VI (note wing-root oil coolers) but was modified by Napier's team at Luton to have an annular radiator (at one time, a ducted spinner).

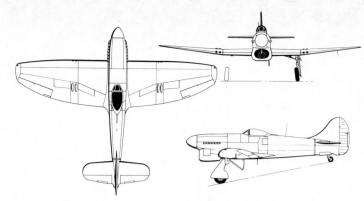

**Above:** Three-view of Hawker Tempest V (post-war, Mk 5).

**Below:** Test-flying a production Tempest V from the Hawker factory at Langley in 1944.

44

# Miles Master and Martinet
## M.9 Master I, M.19 Mk II, M.27 Mk III and M.25 Martinet

**Origin:** Phillips & Powis (Miles Aircraft) Ltd, Woodley, South Marston, Doncaster and Sheffield.

**Type:** Advanced trainer (see text).

**Engine:** (I) 715hp Rolls-Royce Kestrel 30 vee-12; (II) 870hp Bristol Mercury 20 nine-cylinder radial; (III) 825hp Pratt & Whitney R-1535-SB4G Twin Wasp Junior 14-cylinder two-row radial; (Martinet) 870hp Mercury 20 or 30.

**Dimensions:** Span (I) 39ft 0in (11·89m), (some I, all II, III) 35ft 7in or 35ft 9in (10·90m), (M'net) 39ft 1in (11·92m); length (I) 30ft 5in (9·27m), (II) 29ft 6in (8·99m), (III) 30ft 2in (9·20m), (M'net) 30ft 11in (9·425m); height (I) 10ft 0in (3·05m), (II, III) 9ft 3in (2·80m), (M'net) 11ft 7in (3·53m).

**Weights:** Empty (I) 4,308lb (1954kg), (II) 4,130lb (1873kg), (III) 4,210lb (1910kg), (M'net) 4,559lb (2068kg); maximum (I) 5,573lb (2528kg), (II) 5,312lb (2410kg), (III) 5,400lb (2449kg), (M'net) 6,750lb (3062kg).

**Performance:** Maximum speed (I) 226mph (364km/h), (II) 260mph (418km/h), (III) 231mph (372km/h), (M'net) 240mph (386km/h); service ceiling (typical) 27,500ft (8380m); range (typical) 500 miles (805km).

**Armament:** (Most, except Martinet) provision for 0·303in Browning in outer right wing, and for eight practice bombs.

**History:** First flight (Kestrel) 1937, (I) 1938, (production I) March 1939, (II) November 1939, (III) 1940, (Martinet) 24 April 1942.

**Users:** Ireland, Portugal, Turkey, UK (RAF).

**Development:** The brilliant Miles team produced the Kestrel as a private

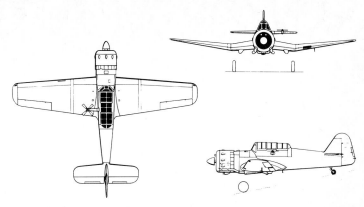

Above: Three-view of Miles M.25 Martinet I.

venture in 1937 to meet an obvious need. After the Air Ministry had spent 18 months trying to buy inferior machines it placed the biggest order for trainers in RAF history, and eventually 900 Master I were delivered. Though 70mph slower than the Kestrel they were ideal in preparing pilots for the new monoplane fighters. Kestrel stocks soon dwindled, and the fastest Master, the Mk II, was urgently planned — only to be held up a year while American engines were imported (for the Master III) in case there were too few Mercuries. Eventually 602 Mk III ran in parallel with 1,747 Mk II, several hundred II being converted in 1942 to tow Hotspur gliders (it involved cropping the bottom of the rudder). The slightly larger and heavier Martinet was the RAF's first purpose-designed tug; 1,724 were built, followed by 66 radio-controlled Queen Martinets. All the Master family were a delight to fly.

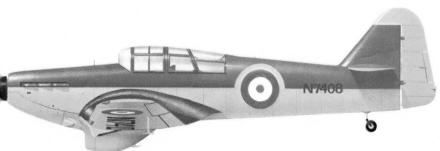

**Left: N7408 was the first production Master I. Later the canopy was made taller, with framed, inclined windscreen.**

**Below: All production Masters had the instructor seated at the rear in a seat which could be elevated. By opening the roof hatch the instructor could then land safely, with good forward vision. This is a Mk III, with the 14-cylinder Twin Wasp Junior. The otherwise similar Mk II had a Mercury, of larger diameter. The airframe was mainly wooden.**

# Short S.25 Sunderland

## Sunderland I, II, III and V (MR.5)

**Origin:** Short Brothers; also built by Blackburn Aircraft.
**Type:** Ocean patrol and anti-submarine flying boat with typical crew of 13.
**Engines:** (I) four 1,010hp Bristol Pegasus 22 nine-cylinder radials; (II, III) four 1,065hp Pegasus XVIII; (V) four 1,200hp Pratt & Whitney R-1830-90B Twin Wasp 14-cylinder two-row radials.
**Dimensions:** Span 112ft 9½in (34·39m); length 85ft 4in (26m); height 32ft 10½in (10·1m).
**Weights:** Empty (III) 34,500lb (15,663kg); (V) 37,000lb (16,783kg); maximum loaded (III) 58,000lb (26,308kg); (V) 60,000lb (27,216kg).
**Performance:** Maximum speed (III, V) 213mph (343km/h); initial climb (III) 720ft (220m)/min; (V) 840ft (256m)/min; service ceiling (typical) 17,400ft (5300m); maximum range (III, V) 2,900 miles (4670km).
**Armament:** (I) eight 0·303in Browning, two in nose turret, four in tail turret and two manually aimed from hatches behind each wing root; internal load of 2,000lb (907kg) of bombs, depth charges, mines and pyrotechnics wound out on rails under inner wing to release position inboard of inner engines; (II, III) as (I) but twin-0·303 in dorsal turret in place of manual guns; (V) as (II, III) with addition in some aircraft of four fixed 0·303in in nose; in many aircraft, also two manually aimed 0·5in Brownings from beam windows, usually in place of dorsal turret.

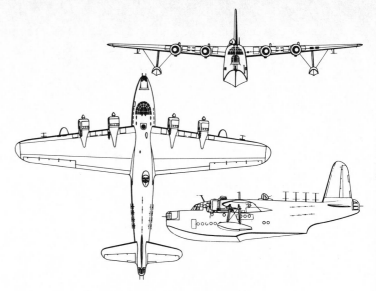

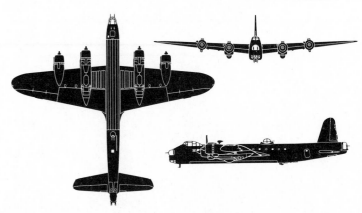

Above: Three-view of Sunderland III (with ASV radar).

# Short S.29 Stirling

## Stirling I to V

**Origin:** Short Brothers, Rochester and Belfast.
**Type:** (I–III) heavy bomber with crew of 7/8; (IV) glider tug and special transport; (V) strategic transport.
**Engines:** (I) four 1,595hp Bristol Hercules XI 14-cylinder sleeve-valve radials; (II) 1,600hp Wright R-2600-A5B Cyclone; (III, IV, V) 1,650hp Bristol Hercules XVI.
**Dimensions:** Span 99ft 1in (30·2m); length (except V) 87ft 3in (26·6m); (V) 90ft 6¾in (27·6m); height 22ft 9in (6·94m).
**Weights:** Empty (I) 44,000lb (19,950kg); (III) 46,900lb (21,273kg); (IV, V, typical) 43,200lb (19,600kg); maximum loaded (I) 59,400lb (26,943kg); (III, IV, V) 70,000lb (31,750kg).
**Performance:** Maximum speed (I–III) 270mph (435km/h); (IV, V) 280mph (451km/h); initial climb (typical) 800ft (244m)/min; service ceiling (I–III) 17,000ft (5182m); range (III) 590 miles (950km) with 14,000lb bombs or 2,010 miles (3235km) with 3,500lb; range (IV, V) 3,000 miles (4828km).
**Armament:** (I) two 0·303in Brownings in nose and dorsal turrets and

Above: Three-view of Stirling I with FN.64 ventral turret.

Below: One of an excellent series of colour photographs taken on a visit to 149 Sqn, one of the first users, in 1941. The immense landing gears gave trouble; the pilot's job was hard.

46

**History:** First flight 16 October 1937; service delivery May 1938; final delivery June 1946.
**Users:** Australia, Norway, South Africa, UK (RAF, BOAC); other countries post-war.

**Development:** Derived from the Imperial Airways Empire flying boat to meet Specification R.2/33, the Sunderland marked a vast improvement in fighting capability over previous biplane boats. From the outbreak of World War II these capacious, reliable and long-ranged boats were ceaselessly at work finding and sinking U-boats, rescuing seamen from sunken vessels and engaging in such fierce battles with enemy aircraft that the Sunderland became known to the Luftwaffe as "Flying Porcupine". Many times single Sunderlands fought off five or more hostile aircraft, and once a Sunderland shot down three of the eight Ju 88s that attacked it and drove off the others. The III introduced an improved planing bottom and, from 1940, all marks carried ASV radar, Leigh lights and an increasing amount of avionics. Altogether 739 were built, 240 by Blackburn at Dumbarton, the Mk III being by far the most numerous. After the war the MR.5 was used on the Berlin Airlift, in Korea, against terrorists in Malaya, on the North Greenland Expedition and by the French Navy and RNZAF. Last sortie was on 15 May 1959 from Singapore, from where Sunderlands had begun combat duty 21 years earlier.

**Left: L2163 was one of the first Mk I Sunderlands, pictured here in 1939 sea-green/purple camouflage and large fin stripes.**

---

our in tail turret, plus (early batches) two in remote control ventral turret; maximum bomb load 18,000lb (8165kg) in fuselage and inner wings; II, III) as (I) but different dorsal turret; (IV) sole armament, tail turret; V) none.
**History:** First flight 14 May 1939; (production Mk I) May 1940; final lelivery (V) November 1945.
**Jser:** UK (RAF).

**Development:** Though extremely impressive, with vast length, unprecedented height and even two separate tailwheels, the Stirling was inpopular. Partly owing to short wing span it had a poor ceiling and sluggish manoeuvrability except at low level. Though it carried a heavy bomb load,

it could not carry bombs bigger than 2,000lb (the largest size when the design was completed in 1938). Operations began with daylight attacks in February 1941, soon switched to night, and by 1943 the Stirling was regarded mainly as a tug and transport and carrier of ECM jamming and spoofing devices for 100 Group. The RAF received 2,221 bomber versions, excluding the two Mk II conversions, and Short's new Belfast plant finally built 160 of the streamlined Mk V transports which carried 40 troops or heavy freight.

**Left: Stirling I of 214 Sqn, based at Stradishall.**

**Below: Last-minute briefing for a Stirling crew before one of the early raids, which were in daylight. Note the tailwheels and original dorsal turret.**

# Supermarine Walrus and Sea Otter

## Walrus I, II; Sea Otter ASR.II

**Origin:** Supermarine Aviation Works (Vickers) Ltd, Southampton; most W and all SO (except prototype) by Saro, East Cowes.

**Type:** Designed as shipboard reconnaissance (see text).

**Engine:** One Bristol nine-cylinder radial, (W I) 620hp Pegasus IIM2 pusher, (W II) 775hp Pegasus VI, (SO) 870hp Mercury 30 tractor.

**Dimensions:** Span (W) 45ft 10in (13·97m), (SO) 46ft 0in; length (W) 37ft 7in (11·45m); (SO) 39ft 4¾in (12·0m); height (land) (W) 15ft 3in (4·65m), (SO) 16ft 2in (4·90m).

**Weights:** Empty (W) 4,900lb (2223kg), (SO) 6,805lb (3087kg); maximum (W) 7,200lb (3266kg), (SO) 10,000lb (4536kg).

**Performance:** Maximum speed (W II) 135mph (217km/h), (SO) 150mph (241km/h); maximum range (W) 600 miles (966km), (SO) 725 miles (1170km).

**History:** First flight (Seagull I) 1922, (Seagull V) 21 June 1933, (Sea Otter) August 1938; final delivery (W) January 1944, (SO) July 1946.

**Users:** (W) Argentina, Australia, Egypt, Ireland, New Zealand, UK (RAF, RN); (SO) UK (RAF, RN).

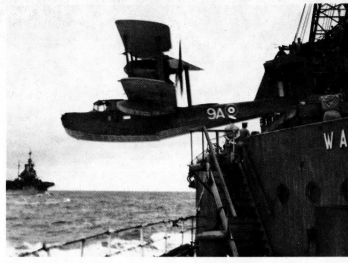

**Above:** A fine 1940 action-shot of a green/purple Walrus leaving the catapult of the battleship Warspite.

**Below:** Three-view of Walrus I with landing gear down.

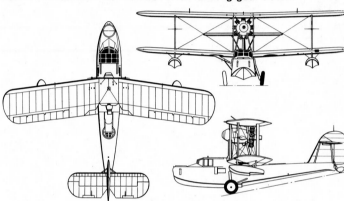

**Development:** Supermarine built various Lion-engined Seagulls in the 1920s and produced the Pegasus-engined Seagull V for the RAAF. In 1935 the name Walrus was given to the Fleet Air Arm three-seater spotter carried by surface warships, with Lewis or Vickers K guns on two open ring mounts and up to 760lb (345kg) bombs or depth charges. Supermarine built 287, followed by 453 wooden-hulled Mk II by Saro. Nearly all served as ASR (air/sea rescue) amphibians, with crew of four; they rescued more than 5,000 aircrew around Britain and the bulk of more than 2,500 in the Mediterranean theatre. The Sea Otter had a fractionally better performance, and two dorsal hatches which when screwed upright formed wind-breaks for three Vickers K. It could get off the water with a much heavier overload, but deliveries did not begin until 5½ years after first flight. Saro built 290, used widely in the Far East. Both amphibians served as utility transports, Admirals' barges and in various electronic and other special roles.

**Below: Air-to-air portrait of a Walrus in early-wartime camouflage. The Walrus was probably the oldest basic aircraft design to participate in the war; it proved extremely useful.**

# Supermarine Spitfire and Seafire

## Mks I to 24 and Seafire I, III, XV, XVII and 45-47

**Origin:** Supermarine Aviation Works (Vickers) Ltd; also built by, Vickers-Armstrongs, Castle Bromwich, and Westland Aircraft; (Seafire) Cunliffe-Owen Aircraft and Westland.

**Type:** Single-seat fighter, fighter-bomber or reconnaissance; (Seafire) carrier-based fighter.

**Engine:** One Rolls-Royce Merlin or Griffon vee-12 liquid-cooled (see text).

**Dimensions:** Span 36ft 10in (11·23m), clipped, 32ft 2in, or, more often, 32ft 7in (9·93m), extended, 40ft 2in (12·24m); length 29ft 11in (9·12m), later, with two-stage engine, typically 31ft 3½in (9·54m), Griffon engine, typically 32ft 8in (9·96m), final (eg Seafire 47) 34ft 4in (10·46m); height 11ft 5in (3·48m), with Griffon, typically 12ft 9in (3·89m).

**Weights:** Empty (Mk I) 4,810lb (2182kg); (IX) 5,610lb (2545kg); (XIV) 6,700lb (3040kg); (Sea.47) 7,625lb (3458kg); maximum loaded (I) 5,784lb (2624kg); (IX) 9,500lb (4310kg); (XIV) 10,280lb (4663kg); Sea.47) 12,750lb (5784kg).

**Performance:** Maximum speed (I) 355–362mph (580km/h); (IX) 408mph (657km/h); (XIV) 448mph (721km/h); (Sea.47) 451mph (724km/h); initial climb (I) 2,530ft (770m)/min; (IX) 4,100ft (1250m)/min; (XIV) 4,580ft (1396m)/min; (Sea.47) 4,800ft (1463m)/min; range on internal fuel (I) 395 miles (637km); (IX) 434 miles (700km); (XIV) 460 miles (740km); (Sea.47) 405 miles (652km).

**Armament:** See text.

**History:** First flight (prototype) 5 March 1936; (production Mk I) July 1938; final delivery (Mk 24) October 1947.

**Users:** (Wartime) Australia, Canada, Czechoslovakia, Egypt, France, Italy (CB), Jugoslavia, Netherlands, Norway, Poland, Portugal, South Africa, Soviet Union, Turkey, UK (RAF, RN), US (AAF).

**Development:** Possibly the most famous combat aircraft in history, the Spitfire was designed by the dying Reginald Mitchell to Specification F.37/34 using the new Rolls-Royce PV.12 engine later named Merlin. It was the first all-metal stressed-skin fighter to go into production in Britain. The following were main versions.

**I** Initial version, 450 ordered in June 1936 with 1,030hp Merlin II, two-blade fixed-pitch propeller and four 0·303in Browning guns. Later Mk IA with eight guns, bulged canopy and three-blade DH v-p propeller and Mk IB with two 20mm Hispano and four 0·303. Production: 1,566.

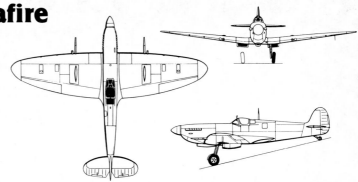

**Above: Three-view of the mass-produced Spitfire IX.**

**II** Mk I built at Castle Bromwich with 1,175hp Merlin·XII and Rotol propeller. Production: 750 IIA (eight 0·303), 170 IIB (two 20mm, four 0·303).

**III** Single experimental model; strengthened Mk I with many changes.

**IV** Confusing because Mk IV was first Griffon-engined, one built. Then unarmed Merlin photo-reconnaissance Mk IV delivered in quantity. Production: 229.

**V** Like PR.IV powered by 1,440hp Merlin 45, many detail changes, main fighter version 1941–42 in three forms: VA, eight 0·303; VB, two 20mm and four 0·303; VC "universal" wing with choice of guns plus two 250lb (113kg) bombs. All with centreline rack for 500lb (227kg) bomb or tank. Many with clipped wings and/or tropical filter under nose. Production: VA, 94; VB, 3,923; VC, 2,447.

**VI** High-altitude interim interceptor, 1,415hp Merlin 47, pressurised cockpit, two 20mm and four 0·303. Production: 100.

**VII** High-altitude, extended wing-tips, new 1,660hp Merlin 61 with two-stage supercharger (and symmetrical underwing radiators); retractable tailwheel, later broad and pointed rudder. Pressurised cockpit. Production: 140.

**VIII** Followed interim Mk IX, virtually unpressurised Mk VII in LF (low-altitude, clipped), F (standard) and HF (high-altitude, extended) versions. Production: 1,658.

▶

**Below: Fine scramble picture of a section of 417 (RCAF) Sqn in Italy, early 1943. The aircraft are tropicalised Spitfire VCs, among the slowest variants ever to be used.**

**IX** Urgent version to counter Fw 190, quick lash-up of V with Merlin 61; again LF, F and HF versions, plus IXE with two 20mm and two 0·5in. Production: 5,665.

**X** Pressurised photo-reconnaissance, Merlin 77, whole leading edge forming fuel tank. Production: 16.

**XI** As X but unpressurised, 1,760hp Merlin 63A or 1,655hp Merlin 70. Mainstay of Photo Reconnaissance Unit 1943–45. Production: 471.

**XII** Low altitude to counter Fw 190 hit-and-run bomber, 1,735hp Griffon III or IV, strengthened VC or VIII airframe, clipped. Production: 100.

**XIII** Low-level reconnaissance, low-rated 1,620hp Merlin 32, four 0·303. Production: 16.

**XIV** First with two-stage Griffon, 2,050hp Mk 65 with deep symmetric radiators and five-blade propeller, completely redesigned airframe with new fuselage, broad fin/rudder, inboard ailerons, retractable tailwheel. F.XIV, two 20mm and four 0·303; F.XIVE, two 20mm and two 0·5in; FR.XIVE, same guns, cut-down rear fuselage and teardrop hood, clipped wings, F.24 camera and extra fuel. Active in 1944, destroyed over 300 flying bombs. Production: 957.

**XVI** As Mk IX but 1,705hp Packard Merlin 266; LF.IXE, E-guns and clipped, many with teardrop hood, extra fuel. Production: 1,054.

**XVIII** Definitive wartime fighter derived from interim XIV, extra fuel, stronger, F and FR versions, some of latter even more fuel and tropical equipment. Production: 300.

**Above: No 92 Sqn was one of the first to receive the Spitfire VB, in March 1941. The Mk V was the most numerous of all (6,464).**

Below: The VB is again the subject of this cutaway, which emphasises the basic simplicity of the structure and the relatively large size of the Hispano 20mm cannon, fed by 60-round drums. Structural heart of the wing was the single spar and strong D-box ahead of it.

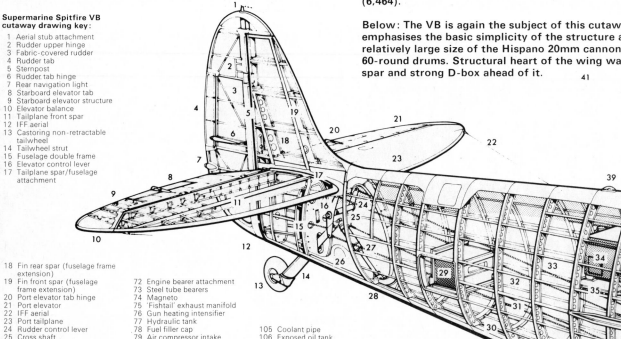

**Supermarine Spitfire VB cutaway drawing key:**

1 Aerial stub attachment
2 Rudder upper hinge
3 Fabric-covered rudder
4 Rudder tab
5 Sternpost
6 Rudder tab hinge
7 Rear navigation light
8 Starboard elevator tab
9 Starboard elevator structure
10 Elevator balance
11 Tailplane front spar
12 IFF aerial
13 Castoring non-retractable tailwheel
14 Tailwheel strut
15 Fuselage double frame
16 Elevator control lever
17 Tailplane spar/fuselage attachment
18 Fin rear spar (fuselage frame extension)
19 Fin front spar (fuselage frame extension)
20 Port elevator tab hinge
21 Port elevator
22 IFF aerial
23 Port tailplane
24 Rudder control lever
25 Cross shaft
26 Tailwheel oleo access plate
27 Tailwheel oleo shock-absorber
28 Fuselage angled frame
29 Battery compartment
30 Lower longeron
31 Elevator control cables
32 Fuselage construction
33 Rudder control cables
34 Radio compartment
35 Radio support tray
36 Flare chute
37 Oxygen bottle
38 Auxiliary long-range fuel tank (29 gal/132 litres)
39 Dorsal formation light
40 Aerial lead-in
41 HF aerial
42 Aerial mast
43 Cockpit aft glazing
44 Voltage regulator
45 Canopy track
46 Structural bulkhead
47 Headrest
48 Perspex canopy
49 Rear-view mirror
50 Entry flap (port)
51 Air bottles (alternative rear fuselage stowage)
52 Sutton harness
53 Pilot's seat (moulded Bakelite)
54 Datum longeron
55 Seat support frame
56 Wing root fillet
57 Seat adjustment lever
58 Rudder pedal frame
59 Elevator control connecting tube
60 Control column spade grip
61 Trim wheel
62 Reflector gunsight
63 External windscreen armour
64 Instrument panel
65 Main fuselage fuel tank (48 gal/218 litres)
66 Fuel tank/longeron attachment fittings
67 Rudder pedals
68 Rudder bar
69 Kingpost
70 Fuselage lower fuel tank (37 gal/168 litres)
71 Firewall/bulkhead
72 Engine bearer attachment
73 Steel tube bearers
74 Magneto
75 'Fishtail' exhaust manifold
76 Gun heating intensifier
77 Hydraulic tank
78 Fuel filler cap
79 Air compressor intake
80 Air compressor
81 Rolls-Royce Merlin 45 or 50 series 12-cylinder engine, 1,470 hp
82 Coolant piping
83 Port cannon magazine fairing
84 Flaps
85 Aileron control cables
86 Aileron push tube
87 Bellcrank
88 Aileron hinge
89 Port aileron
90 Machine-gun access panels
91 Port wingtip
92 Port navigation light
93 Leading-edge skinning
94 Machine-gun ports (protected)
95 Port wing cannon
96 Three-blade constant-speed propeller (Rotol or DH)
97 Spinner
98 Propeller hub
99 Coolant tank
100 Cowling fastening
101 Engine anti-vibration mounting pad
102 Engine accessories
103 Engine bearers
104 Main engine support member
105 Coolant pipe
106 Exposed oil tank
107 Port mainwheel
108 Mainwheel fairing
109 Carburettor air intake
110 Stub/spar attachment
111 Mainwheel leg pivot point
112 Main spar
113 Leading-edge ribs (diagonals deleted for clarity)
114 Mainwheel leg shock-absorber
115 Mainwheel fairing
116 Starboard mainwheel
117 Angled axle
118 Hispano 20mm cannon barrel support fairing
119 Spar cut-out
120 Mainwheel well
121 Gun heating pipe
122 Flap structure
123 Cannon magazine fairing
124 Cannon magazine drum (60 rounds)
125 Machine-gun support brackets
126 Gun access panels
127 Browning 0·303in machine-gun barrels
128 Machine-gun ports
129 Ammunition boxes (350 rpg)
130 Starboard aileron construction
131 Wing ribs
132 Single-tube outer spar section
133 Wingtip structure
134 Starboard navigation light

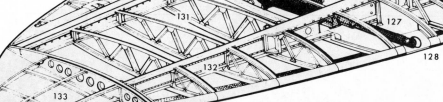

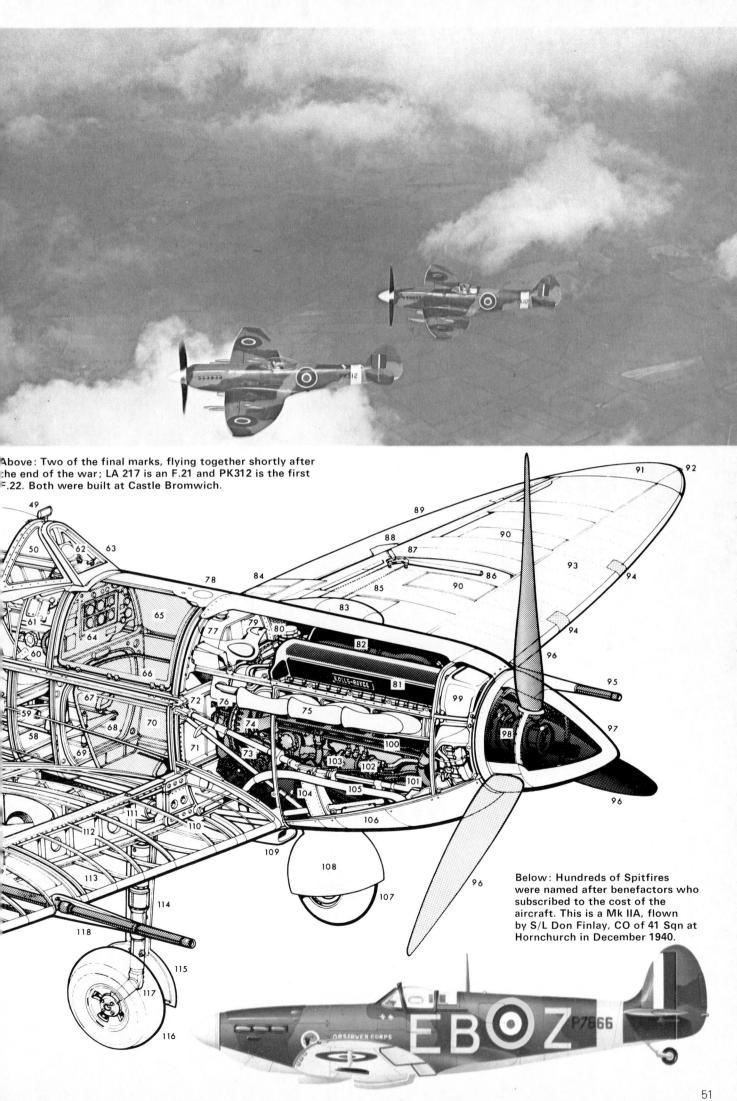

Above: Two of the final marks, flying together shortly after the end of the war; LA 217 is an F.21 and PK312 is the first F.22. Both were built at Castle Bromwich.

Below: Hundreds of Spitfires were named after benefactors who subscribed to the cost of the aircraft. This is a Mk IIA, flown by S/L Don Finlay, CO of 41 Sqn at Hornchurch in December 1940.

51

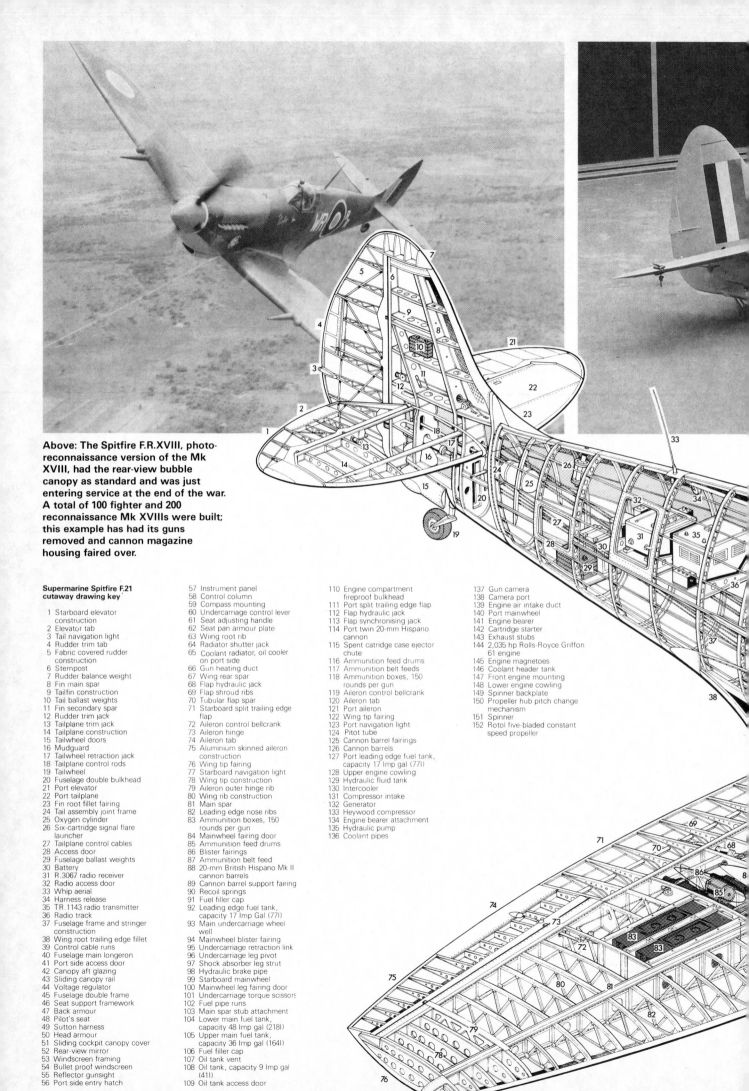

**Above: The Spitfire F.R.XVIII, photo-reconnaissance version of the Mk XVIII, had the rear-view bubble canopy as standard and was just entering service at the end of the war. A total of 100 fighter and 200 reconnaissance Mk XVIIIs were built; this example has had its guns removed and cannon magazine housing faired over.**

**Supermarine Spitfire F.21 cutaway drawing key**

1 Starboard elevator construction
2 Elevator tab
3 Tail navigation light
4 Rudder trim tab
5 Fabric covered rudder construction
6 Sternpost
7 Rudder balance weight
8 Fin main spar
9 Tailfin construction
10 Tail ballast weights
11 Fin secondary spar
12 Rudder trim jack
13 Tailplane trim jack
14 Tailplane construction
15 Tailwheel doors
16 Mudguard
17 Tailwheel retraction jack
18 Tailplane control rods
19 Tailwheel
20 Fuselage double bulkhead
21 Port elevator
22 Port tailplane
23 Fin root fillet fairing
24 Tail assembly joint frame
25 Oxygen cylinder
26 Six-cartridge signal flare launcher
27 Tailplane control cables
28 Access door
29 Fuselage ballast weights
30 Battery
31 R.3067 radio receiver
32 Radio access door
33 Whip aerial
34 Harness release
35 TR.1143 radio transmitter
36 Radio track
37 Fuselage frame and stringer construction
38 Wing root trailing edge fillet
39 Control cable runs
40 Fuselage main longeron
41 Port side access door
42 Canopy aft glazing
43 Sliding canopy rail
44 Voltage regulator
45 Fuselage double frame
46 Seat support framework
47 Back armour
48 Pilot's seat
49 Sutton harness
50 Head armour
51 Sliding cockpit canopy cover
52 Rear-view mirror
53 Windscreen framing
54 Bullet proof windscreen
55 Reflector gunsight
56 Port side entry hatch

57 Instrument panel
58 Control column
59 Compass mounting
60 Undercarriage control lever
61 Seat adjusting handle
62 Seat pan armour plate
63 Wing root rib
64 Radiator shutter jack
65 Coolant radiator, oil cooler on port side
66 Gun heating duct
67 Wing rear spar
68 Flap hydraulic jack
69 Flap shroud ribs
70 Tubular flap spar
71 Starboard split trailing edge flap
72 Aileron control bellcrank
73 Aileron hinge
74 Aileron tab
75 Aluminium skinned aileron construction
76 Wing tip fairing
77 Starboard navigation light
78 Wing tip construction
79 Aileron outer hinge rib
80 Wing rib construction
81 Main spar
82 Leading edge nose ribs
83 Ammunition boxes, 150 rounds per gun
84 Mainwheel fairing door
85 Ammunition feed drums
86 Blister fairings
87 Ammunition belt feed
88 20-mm British Hispano Mk II cannon barrels
89 Cannon barrel support fairing
90 Recoil springs
91 Fuel filler cap
92 Leading edge fuel tank, capacity 17 Imp Gal (77l)
93 Main undercarriage wheel well
94 Mainwheel blister fairing
95 Undercarriage retraction link
96 Undercarriage leg pivot
97 Shock absorber leg strut
98 Hydraulic brake pipe
99 Starboard mainwheel
100 Mainwheel leg fairing door
101 Undercarriage torque scissors
102 Fuel pipe runs
103 Main spar stub attachment
104 Lower main fuel tank, capacity 48 Imp gal (218l)
105 Upper main fuel tank, capacity 36 Imp gal (164l)
106 Fuel filler cap
107 Oil tank vent
108 Oil tank, capacity 9 Imp gal (41l)
109 Oil tank access door

110 Engine compartment fireproof bulkhead
111 Port split trailing edge flap
112 Flap hydraulic jack
113 Flap synchronising jack
114 Port twin 20-mm Hispano cannon
115 Spent catridge case ejector chute
116 Ammunition feed drums
117 Ammunition belt feeds
118 Ammunition boxes, 150 rounds per gun
119 Aileron control bellcrank
120 Aileron tab
121 Port aileron
122 Wing tip fairing
123 Port navigation light
124 Pitot tube
125 Cannon barrel fairings
126 Cannon barrels
127 Port leading edge fuel tank, capacity 17 Imp gal (77l)
128 Upper engine cowling
129 Hydraulic fluid tank
130 Intercooler
131 Compressor intake
132 Generator
133 Heywood compressor
134 Engine bearer attachment
135 Hydraulic pump
136 Coolant pipes

137 Gun camera
138 Camera port
139 Engine air intake duct
140 Port mainwheel
141 Engine bearer
142 Cartridge starter
143 Exhaust stubs
144 2,035 hp Rolls-Royce Griffon 61 engine
145 Engine magnetoes
146 Coolant header tank
147 Front engine mounting
148 Lower engine cowling
149 Spinner backplate
150 Propeller hub pitch change mechanism
151 Spinner
152 Rotol five-bladed constant speed propeller

Above: The final production version of the Spitfire was the F.24, with 2,400hp Griffon 61 engine, five-blade propeller and short-barrel cannon. This example is shown in postwar service with the Royal Hong Kong Auxiliary Air Force.

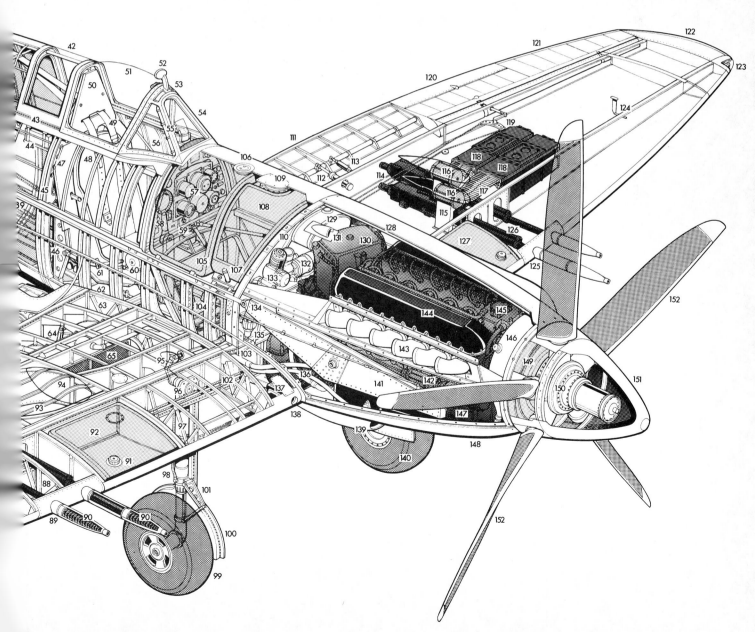

**XIX** Final photo-reconnaissance, 2,050hp Griffon 65 and unpressurised, then Griffon 66 with pressure cabin and increased wing tankage; both option of deep slipper tank for 1,800 mile (2900km) range. Made last RAF Spitfire sortie, Malaya, 1 April 1954. Production: 225.

**21** Post-war, redesigned aircraft with different structure and shape, 2,050hp Griffon 65 or 85, four 20mm and 1,000lb (454kg) bombs. Production: 122.

**22** Bubble hood, 24-volt electrics, some with 2,375hp Griffon 65 and contraprop. Production: 278.

**24** Redesigned tail, short-barrel cannon, zero-length rocket launchers. Production: 54. Total Spitfire production 20,334.

**Seafire IB** Navalised Spitfire VB, usually 1,415hp low-rated Merlin 46. Fixed wings but hook and slinging points. Conversions: 166.

**IIC** Catapult spools, strengthened landing gear, 1,645hp Merlin 32 and four-blade propeller. Various sub-types, Universal wing. Production: 262 Supermarine, 110 Westland.

**III** Manual double-fold wing, 1,585hp Merlin 55M, various versions. Production: 870 Westland, 350 Cunliffe-Owen.

**XV** (Later F.15) 1,850hp Griffon VI, four-blade, asymmetric radiators, cross between Seafire III and Spitfire XII. Production: 390.

**XVII** (F.17) Increased fuel, cut-down fuselage and bubble hood. Production: (cut by war's end): 232.

**45** New aircraft entirely, corresponding to Spitfire 21; Griffon 61 (five-blade) or 85 (contraprop); fixed wing, four 20mm. Production: 50.

**46** Bubble hood like Spitfire 22. Production: 24.

**47** Navalised Spitfire 24, hydraulically folding wings, carb-air intake just behind propeller, increased fuel. Fought in Malaya and Korea. Production: 140. Total Seafires: 2,556.

**Right: An unusual angle on a Spitfire VB rolling towards the photographic aircraft. There were no tabs on the ailerons, but there was one on each tail control surface.**

**Below: BL479 was yet another Spitfire VB, but a much later one than those in other illustrations. It had the LF (low-altitude fighter) clipped wing used on several other Merlin marks.**

# Vickers Vildebeest and Vincent

## Vildebeest I to IV and Vincent (Types 267, 286 and 266)

**Origin:** Vickers (Aviation) Ltd.
**Type:** (Vildebeest) torpedo bomber with crew of three (IV, two); (Vincent) three-seat general purpose.
**Engine:** One 660hp Bristol Pegasus IIM3 nine-cylinder radial (Spanish CASA-built Vildebeest) 595hp Hispano 12Nbr; (Vildebeest IV) 825hp Bristol Perseus VIII nine-cylinder sleeve-valve radial.
**Dimensions:** Span 49ft (14·94m); length 36ft 8in (11·17m); (Vildebeest IV) 37ft 8in; height 17ft 9in (5·42m).
**Weights:** Empty 4,229lb (1918kg); (Vildebeest IV) 4,724lb; maximum loaded 8,100lb (3674kg); (Vildebeest IV) 8,500lb.
**Performance:** Maximum speed 142mph (230km/h); (Vildebeest IV) 156mph; initial climb 765ft (233m)/min; service ceiling 17,000ft (5182m); range 1,250 miles (2000km).
**Armament:** One 0·303in Vickers fixed firing forward, one 0·303in Lewis manually aimed from rear cockpit; external bomb load of 1,000lb (454kg) or (Vildebeest) one 18in (457mm) torpedo.
**History:** First flight (Vildebeest) April 1928; service delivery (Vildebeest I) April 1933; (Vincent) late 1934; final delivery (Vildebeest IV) November 1937.
**Users:** UK (RAF); briefly Australia and New Zealand.

**Development:** Designed to replace the Horsley as the RAF's coastal-defence torpedo-bomber, the Vildebeest (originally Vildebeeste) appeared with an uncowled Jupiter engine and two widely separated cockpits, the pilot being just ahead of the rectangular slatted wings and having a superb view. The production Mk I had a third cockpit and early Pegasus engine. After building 176, Vickers delivered 18 Mk IV with the first sleeve-valve

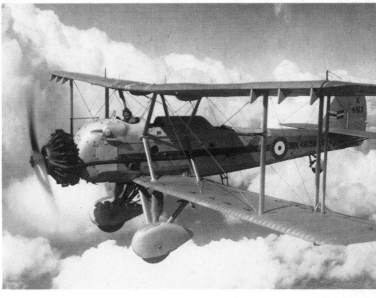

Above: K4163 was a Vildebeest III. Large and surprisingly capable, the Vildebeest was not totally obsolete at the start of World War II and saw much valiant action.

engines ever cleared for service, fully cowled and driving three-blade Rotol propellers. In 1939 the Vildebeest was the RAF's only torpedo carrier, and in 1941 Nos 36 and 100 Sqns at Singapore fought alone to try to hold back the Japanese, the last two aircraft surviving until March 1942 in Sumatra. The later Vincent, of which 171 were built between 1934 and 1936, served throughout the Middle East and Africa until 1942. One of its main replacements was the aircraft described below.

# Vickers Wellesley

## Type 287, Wellesley I and II

**Origin:** Vickers (Aviation) Ltd.
**Type:** Two-seat general-purpose bomber.
**Engine:** One 925hp Bristol Pegasus XX nine-cylinder radial.
**Dimensions:** Span 74ft 7in (22·73m); length 39ft 3in (11·96m); height 12ft 4in (3·75m).
**Weights:** Empty 6,369lb (2889kg); maximum loaded (except record flight) 11,100lb (5035kg).
**Performance:** Maximum speed 228mph (369km/h); initial climb 1,200ft (366m)/min; service ceiling 33,000ft (10,060m); range with bomb load 1,110 miles (1786km).
**Armament:** One 0·303in belt-fed Vickers in right wing firing ahead, one Vickers K manually aimed from rear cockpit; four 500lb (227kg) or eight 250lb bombs in streamlined containers, originally fitted with bomb doors, under wings.
**History:** First flight 19 June 1935; service delivery April 1937; final delivery May 1938.
**User:** UK (RAF), possibly passed on to other Middle East countries.

**Development:** Vickers built a large biplane to meet the RAF G.4/31 specification, but it was so humdrum the company board decided at their own risk to build a monoplane using the radical geodetic (metal basketwork) construction developed for airships by their structural wizard B.N. (later Sir Barnes) Wallis. The result was so dramatically superior the Air Ministry lost its fear of monoplanes and bought 176 as the Wellesley. Distinguished by great span, high aspect ratio, extreme cruise efficiency and a most reliable engine (identical in size to the Jupiter but of virtually twice the power) it was natural to form a special Long-Range Development Flight. Three aircraft, with three seats, extra fuel and long-chord cowlings, took off from Ismailia, Egypt, on 5 November 1938; one landed at Koepang and the other two reached Darwin, 7,162 miles (11,525km) in 48 hours non-stop. In World War II Wellesleys were extremely active in East Africa, Egypt, the Middle East and surrounding sea areas until late 1942.

Above: The Wellesley saw most of its service in east and north-east Africa in 1940-42. This example, pictured in 1940, has the hood of the rear cockpit swung open and the gun ready for action. The containers housed the bombs.

Left: One of the very first Wellesleys to reach the RAF was this example delivered to 76 Sqn at RAF Finningley, Yorkshire, in April 1937.

# Vickers-Armstrongs Wellington

## Type 415 and 440, Wellington I to T.19

**Origin:** Vickers-Armstrongs (Aircraft) Ltd.
**Type:** Originally long-range bomber with crew of six; later, see text.
**Engines:** Variously two Bristol Pegasus nine-cylinder radials, two Rolls-Royce Merlin vee-12 liquid-cooled, two Pratt & Whitney Twin Wasp 14-cylinder two-row radials or two Bristol Hercules 14-cylinder two-row sleeve-valve radials; for details see text.
**Dimensions:** Span 86ft 2in (26·26m); (V, VI) 98ft 2in; length (most) 64ft 7in (19·68m), (some, 60ft 10in or, with Leigh light, 66ft); height 17ft 6in (5·33m), (some 17ft).
**Weights:** Empty (IC) 18,556lb (8417kg); (X) 26,325lb (11,940kg); maximum loaded (IC) 25,800lb (11,703kg); (III) 29,500lb (13,381kg) (X) 36,500lb (16,556kg).
**Performance:** Maximum speed (IC) 235mph (379km/h); (most other marks) 247—256mph (410km/h); (V, VI) 300mph (483km/h); initial climb (all, typical) 1,050ft (320m)/min; service ceiling (bomber versions

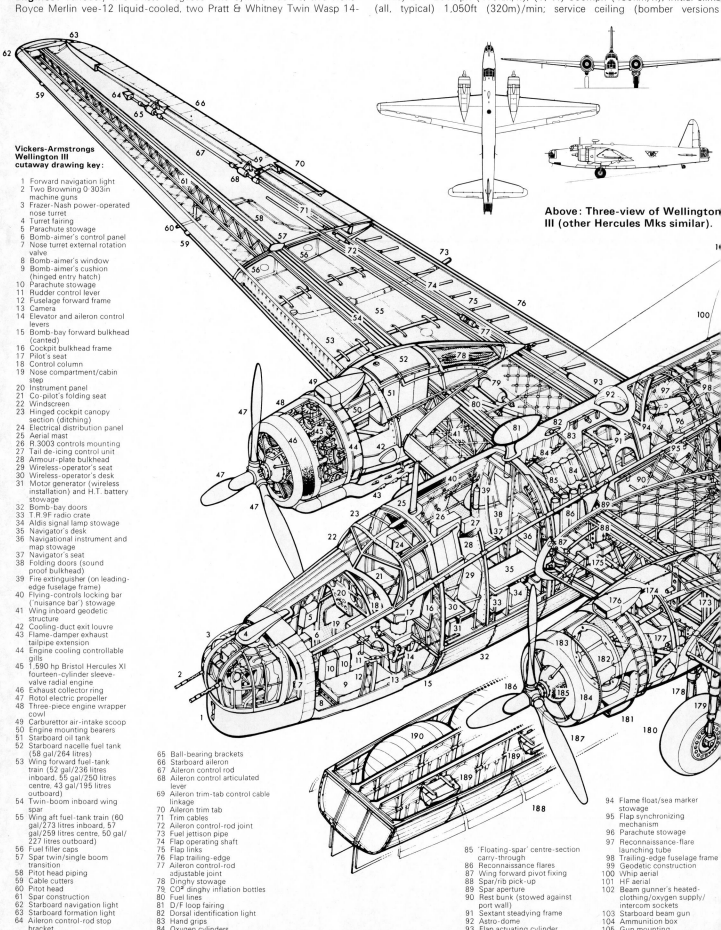

**Above: Three-view of Wellington III (other Hercules Mks similar).**

### Vickers-Armstrongs Wellington III cutaway drawing key:

1 Forward navigation light
2 Two Browning 0·303in machine guns
3 Frazer-Nash power-operated nose turret
4 Turret fairing
5 Parachute stowage
6 Bomb-aimer's control panel
7 Nose turret external rotation valve
8 Bomb-aimer's window
9 Bomb-aimer's cushion (hinged entry hatch)
10 Parachute stowage
11 Rudder control lever
12 Fuselage forward frame
13 Camera
14 Elevator and aileron control levers
15 Bomb-bay forward bulkhead (canted)
16 Cockpit bulkhead frame
17 Pilot's seat
18 Control column
19 Nose compartment/cabin step
20 Instrument panel
21 Co-pilot's folding seat
22 Windscreen
23 Hinged cockpit canopy section (ditching)
24 Electrical distribution panel
25 Aerial mast
26 R.3003 controls mounting
27 Tail de-icing control unit
28 Armour-plate bulkhead
29 Wireless-operator's seat
30 Wireless-operator's desk
31 Motor generator (wireless installation) and H.T. battery stowage
32 Bomb-bay doors
33 T.R.9F radio crate
34 Aldis signal lamp stowage
35 Navigator's desk
36 Navigational instrument and map stowage
37 Navigator's seat
38 Folding doors (sound proof bulkhead)
39 Fire extinguisher (on leading-edge fuselage frame)
40 Flying-controls locking bar ('nuisance bar') stowage
41 Wing inboard geodetic structure
42 Cooling-duct exit louvre
43 Flame-damper exhaust tailpipe extension
44 Engine cooling controllable gills
45 1,590 hp Bristol Hercules XI fourteen-cylinder sleeve-valve radial engine
46 Exhaust collector ring
47 Rotol electric propeller
48 Three-piece engine wrapper cowl
49 Carburettor air-intake scoop
50 Engine mounting bearers
51 Starboard oil tank
52 Starboard nacelle fuel tank (58 gal/264 litres)
53 Wing forward fuel-tank train (52 gal/236 litres inboard, 55 gal/250 litres centre, 43 gal/195 litres outboard)
54 Twin-boom inboard wing spar
55 Wing aft fuel-tank train (60 gal/273 litres inboard, 57 gal/259 litres centre, 50 gal/227 litres outboard)
56 Fuel filler caps
57 Spar twin/single boom transition
58 Pitot head piping
59 Cable cutters
60 Pitot head
61 Spar construction
62 Starboard navigation light
63 Starboard formation light
64 Aileron control-rod stop bracket

65 Ball-bearing brackets
66 Starboard aileron
67 Aileron control rod
68 Aileron control articulated lever
69 Aileron trim-tab control cable linkage
70 Aileron trim tab
71 Trim cables
72 Aileron control-rod joint
73 Fuel jettison pipe
74 Flap operating shaft
75 Flap links
76 Flap trailing-edge
77 Aileron control-rod adjustable joint
78 Dinghy stowage
79 CO² dinghy inflation bottles
80 Fuel lines
81 D/F loop fairing
82 Dorsal identification light
83 Hand grips
84 Oxygen cylinders

85 'Floating-spar' centre-section carry-through
86 Reconnaissance flares
87 Whip forward pivot fixing
88 Spar/rib pick-up
89 Spar aperture
90 Rest bunk (stowed against port wall)
91 Sextant steadying frame
92 Astro-dome
93 Flap actuating cylinder
94 Flame float/sea marker stowage
95 Flap synchronizing mechanism
96 Parachute stowage
97 Reconnaissance-flare launching tube
98 Trailing-edge fuselage frame
99 Geodetic construction
100 Whip aerial
101 HF aerial
102 Beam gunner's heated-clothing/oxygen supply/intercom sockets
103 Starboard beam gun
104 Ammunition box
105 Gun mounting

typical) 22,000ft (6710m); (V, VI) 38,000ft (11,600m); range with weapon load of 1,500lb (680kg), typically 2,200 miles (3540km).
**Armament:** See text.
**History:** First flight (B.9/32) 15 June 1936; (production Mk I) 23 December 1937; service delivery (I) October 1938; final delivery (T.10) 13 October 1945.
**Users:** (Wartime) Australia, Czechoslovakia, France, New Zealand, Poland, UK (RAF).

**Below:** The subject of the cutaway is the most important "Wimpey", the Mk III, which continued to be a mainstay of Bomber Command after the entry to service of the more capable four-engined heavies.

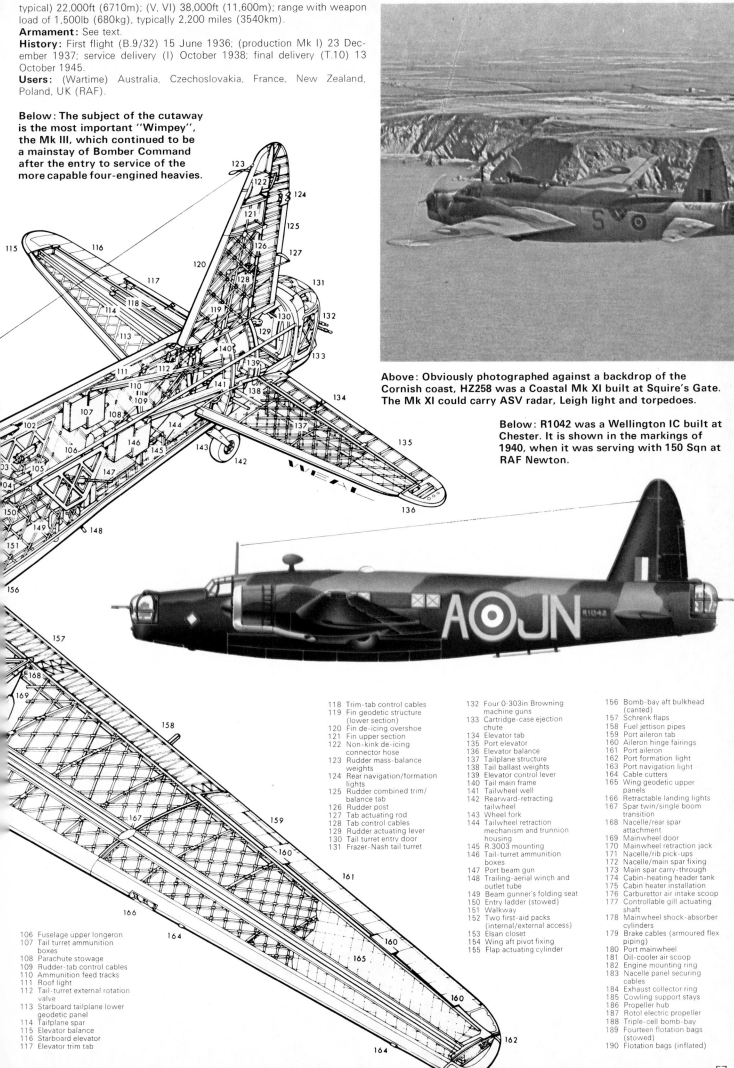

**Above:** Obviously photographed against a backdrop of the Cornish coast, HZ258 was a Coastal Mk XI built at Squire's Gate. The Mk XI could carry ASV radar, Leigh light and torpedoes.

**Below:** R1042 was a Wellington IC built at Chester. It is shown in the markings of 1940, when it was serving with 150 Sqn at RAF Newton.

106 Fuselage upper longeron
107 Tail turret ammunition boxes
108 Parachute stowage
109 Rudder-tab control cables
110 Ammunition feed tracks
111 Roof light
112 Tail-turret external rotation valve
113 Starboard tailplane lower geodetic panel
114 Tailplane spar
115 Elevator balance
116 Starboard elevator
117 Elevator trim tab

118 Trim-tab control cables
119 Fin geodetic structure (lower section)
120 Fin de-icing overshoe
121 Fin upper section
122 Non-kink de-icing connector hose
123 Rudder mass-balance weights
124 Rear navigation/formation lights
125 Rudder combined trim/balance tab
126 Rudder post
127 Tab actuating rod
128 Tab control cables
129 Rudder actuating lever
130 Tail turret entry door
131 Frazer-Nash tail turret

132 Four 0·303in Browning machine guns
133 Cartridge-case ejection chute
134 Elevator tab
135 Port elevator
136 Elevator balance
137 Tailplane structure
138 Tail ballast weights
139 Elevator control lever
140 Tail main frame
141 Tailwheel well
142 Rearward-retracting tailwheel
143 Wheel fork
144 Tailwheel retraction mechanism and trunnion housing
145 R.3003 mounting
146 Tail-turret ammunition boxes
147 Port beam gun
148 Trailing-aerial winch and outlet tube
149 Beam gunner's folding seat
150 Entry ladder (stowed)
151 Walkway
152 Two first-aid packs (internal/external access)
153 Elsan closet
154 Wing aft pivot fixing
155 Flap actuating cylinder

156 Bomb-bay aft bulkhead (canted)
157 Schrenk flaps
158 Fuel jettison pipes
159 Port aileron tab
160 Aileron hinge fairings
161 Port aileron
162 Port formation light
163 Port navigation light
164 Cable cutters
165 Wing geodetic upper panels
166 Retractable landing lights
167 Spar twin/single boom transition
168 Nacelle/rear spar attachment
169 Mainwheel door
170 Mainwheel retraction jack
171 Nacelle/rib pick-ups
172 Nacelle/main spar fixing
173 Main spar carry-through
174 Cabin-heating header tank
175 Cabin heater installation
176 Carburettor air intake scoop
177 Controllable gill actuating shaft
178 Mainwheel shock-absorber cylinders
179 Brake cables (armoured flex piping)
180 Port mainwheel
181 Oil-cooler air scoop
182 Engine mounting ring
183 Nacelle panel securing cables
184 Exhaust collector ring
185 Cowling support stays
186 Propeller hub
187 Rotol electric propeller
188 Triple-cell bomb-bay
189 Fourteen flotation bags (stowed)
190 Flotation bags (inflated)

► **Development:** It was natural that Vickers (Aviation), from October 1938 Vickers-Armstrongs (Aicraft), should have followed up the success of the Wellesley with a larger bomber using the geodetic form of construction. There were difficulties in applying it to wings, cut-out nacelles and fuselages with large bomb-doors and turrets, but the B.9/32 prototype was obviously efficient, and by September 1939 had been developed into Britain's most formidable bomber. The following were chief versions:

**I** Powered by 1,050hp Pegasus XVIII and originally with twin 0·303in Brownings in simple Vickers turrets at nose and tail; internal bomb load 4,500lb (2041kg). Built one-a-day at Weybridge, later a further 50 per month at Chester and, later still, about 30 a month at Squire's Gate, Blackpool. Mk IA had Nash and Thompson power turrets, and the main IC version had two beam guns (some earlier had a ventral barbette). Production: 180+ 183+ 2,685.

**II** Had 1,145hp Merlin X, otherwise as IC. Production: 400.

**III** Main Bomber Command type in 1941–2, with 1,375hp Hercules III or XI, and four-gun tail turret. Production: 1,519.

**IV** Flown by two Polish squadrons, powered by 1,200hp Twin Wasp R-1830-S3C4-G. Production: 220.

**V** Experimental pressurised high-altitude, turbocharged Hercules VIII. Three built, converted to VI.

**VI** Long-span pressurised, with 1,600hp Merlin R6SM engines, no guns and special equipment. Used by 109 Sqn and as Gee trainers. Production 63.

**VII** One only, Merlin engines, tested large 40mm Vickers S gun turret for P.92 fighter, later with twin guns.

**VIII** Conversion of IC as Coastal reconnaissance version, with ASV radar arrays, Leigh light in long nose, and two 18in torpedoes or anti-submarine weapons. Some, huge hoops for detonating magnetic mines.

**IX** Conversion of IC for special trooping.

**X** Standard bomber, similar to III but 1,675hp Hercules VI or XVI. Peak production rate per month in 1942 was Weybridge 70, Chester 130 and Blackpool 102. Production: 3,804.

**XI** Advanced Coastal version of X, no mast aerials but large chin radome, torpedoes, retractable Leigh light.

**XII** Similar to XI, with Leigh light ventral.

**XIII** Reverted to ASV Mk II with masts, and nose turret.

**XIV** Final Coastal, ASV.III chin radome, wing rocket rails, Leigh light in bomb bay.

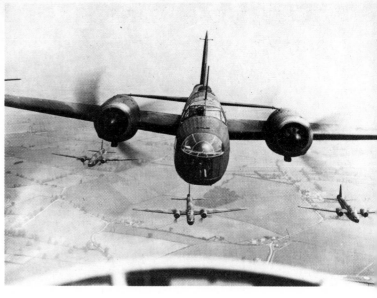

Above: These early Mk I Wellingtons were photographed participating in exercises shortly before the outbreak of war.

**XV, XVI** Unarmed Transport Command conversions of IC.

Total production of this outstanding type amounted to 11,461. After World War II hundreds were converted for use as trainers, the main variant being the T.10 which remained in service until 1953. The T.19 was a specialised navigation trainer. The Vickers successor to the Wellington, the bigger, Warwick, was inferior to four-engine machines, and was used mainly in Coastal and transport roles.

Below: A Polish corporal looks out of the right flight-deck window of a "Wimpey" with an obviously impressive ops record.

# Vickers-Armstrongs Warwick

## Type 462 (ASR.I), 460 (C.III), 473 (GR.V)

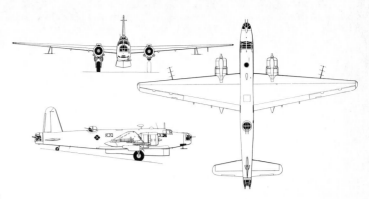

**Origin:** Vickers-Armstrongs Ltd, Weybridge.
**Type:** Designed as bomber (see text).
**Engines:** Two 18-cylinder radials, (I, III) 1,850hp Pratt & Whitney R-2800-S1A4G or -2SBG, (II, V) 2,520hp Bristol Centaurus VII sleeve-valve.
**Dimensions:** Span 96ft 8½in (29·48m); length (all) 72ft 5in to 72ft 11in (22·20m); height 18ft 6in (5·64m).
**Weights:** Empty (I) 28,154lb (12,701kg), (V) 31,230lb (14,226kg); maximum (I) 45,000lb (20,412kg), (III) 46,000lb (20,865kg), (V) 50,000lb (22,680kg).
**Performance:** Maximum speed (I) 224mph (360km/h), (III) 250mph (402km/h), (V) 295mph (475km/h); maximum range with full load (I) 2,300 miles (3700km), (III) 2,150 miles (3459km), (V) 3,052 miles (4911km).
**History:** First flight 13 August 1939, (production B.I) January 1942; service delivery (civil III) February 1943, (ASR.I) May 1943, (GR.V) June 1945.
**User:** UK (RAF, BOAC).

**Development:** Designed as a successor to the Wellington to B.1/35, the Warwick was potentially an outstanding aircraft, despite its geodetic/fabric construction, but its career was marred by continual indecision and by unavailability of properly developed engines. The Vultures used at first flight were hopeless, and eventually 16 B.I were delivered with Double Wasp R-2800 engines but used for research and trials. The ASR.I had the same engines and 369 were delivered carrying Lindholme parachuted survival gear, a Mk I lifeboat and, later, ASV radar, a Mk II lifeboat and various armament including eight 0·303in in three turrets. The C.I was an unarmed transport, while the C.III had better nose and tail fairings and carried a freight pannier in the bomb bay. A vast improvement in stability came with a revised rudder and added dorsal fin, and in performance with a switch to Centaurus engines. The GR.II, 133 of which were built, served as a reconnaissance and multi-role machine in the UK and Mediterranean, but the completely redesigned GR.V just missed the war. With Leigh light instead of a dorsal turret, and 0·5in guns, this fine aircraft served in Coastal Command post-war. Though today mistakenly regarded as a near-failure, the 700-odd Warwicks worked hard during the war and among other things were the chief ASR landplanes, the chief carriers of mail, and as utility transports second only to the Dakota.

**Above: Three-view of Warwick ASR.I with lifeboat and radar.**

**Below: Powered by Double Wasps, the Warwick C.III was a most useful and widely used transport, yet never in the limelight.**

# Westland Lysander

## Lysander I, II, III and IIIA versions

**Origin:** Westland Aircraft Ltd; also built by National Steel Car Corporation, Malton, Toronto.
**Type:** Two-seat army co-operation; later, see text.
**Engine:** One Bristol nine-cylinder radial; (I) 890hp Mercury XII; (II) 905hp Perseus XII sleeve-valve; (III) 870hp Mercury XX or XXX.
**Dimensions:** Span 50ft (15·24m); length 30ft 6in (9·29m); height 11ft 6in (3·50m).
**Weights:** Empty (typical I) 4,044lb (1834kg); normal loaded (I) 5,833lb (2645kg); maximum loaded (I) 7,500lb (3402kg); (IIISCW) 10,000lb (4536kg).
**Performance:** Maximum speed (I, II) 237mph (381km/h); (IIISCW) 190mph (306km/h); initial climb (I) 1,900ft (580m)/min; service ceiling (I) 26,000ft (7925m); range (I) 600 miles (966km); (IIISCW) 1,400 miles (2253km).
**Armament:** When fitted, one 0·303in Browning, with 500 rounds, above each wheel spat (outside propeller disc) and one 0·303in Lewis or Vickers GO manually aimed from rear cockpit (IIIA, twin 0·303in Browning in rear cockpit); bomb load up to two 250lb (113kg) on stub wings, or 16 20lb (9kg), four on fuselage carrier.
**History:** First flight 15 June 1936; service delivery June 1938; final delivery (Westland) January 1942, (Canada) late 1942.
**Users:** Canada, Egypt, Ireland, Turkey, UK (RAF, RN).

**Development:** One of the most distinctive military aircraft, the STOL Lysander was designed to A.39/34 as an army co-operation machine. When 16 Sqn at Old Sarum received the type in 1938 it practised sedate picking up of messages and spotting for artillery. When war came, however, the well-liked "Lizzie" blossomed forth as a remarkable multi-role aircraft. The first He 111 to be shot down in BEF territory (in November 1939) fell to a Lysander's modest armament, and in June 1940 some served as night fighters whilst others spent their time in fierce ground attack on the German army and making precision supply-drops to the defenders of Calais. During the rest of the war Lysanders served as target tugs, overseas close support, air/sea rescue and, memorably, in IIISCW form for dropping agents in Europe and recovering special passengers for Britain. The heavily loaded SCW had a belly tank, much special gear and a vital ladder to give access to the lofty cockpit. Production by Westland was 1,425, some of which were grotesque experimental versions; 325 more were built in Canada. In 1974, after years of work, a Californian restored one to flying condition.

# Westland Whirlwind

## Whirlwind I, IA

**Origin:** Westland Aircraft Ltd.
**Type:** Single-seat day fighter (later fighter-bomber).
**Engines:** Two 885hp Rolls-Royce Peregrine I vee-12 liquid-cooled.
**Dimensions:** Span 45ft (13·72m); length 32ft 9in (9·98m); height 11ft 7in (3·52m).
**Weights:** Empty (I) 7,840lb (3699kg); (IA) 8,310lb (3770kg); maximum loaded 10,270lb (4658kg); (IA) 11,388lb (5166kg).
**Performance:** Maximum speed (clean) 360mph (580km/h), (with bombs) 270mph (435km/h); initial climb (clean) 3,000ft (915m)/min; service ceiling (clean) 30,000ft (9144m); range, not recorded but about 800 miles (1290km).
**Armament:** Standard, four 20mm Hispano Mk I cannon in nose, each with 60-round drum; IA added underwing racks for bomb load up to 1,000lb (454kg).
**History:** First flight 11 October 1938; service delivery June 1940; final delivery December 1941.
**User:** UK (RAF).

**Development:** At the outbreak of World War II the gravest deficiency of the RAF was in the field of twin-engined high-performance machines for use as long-range escort or night fighters. This was precisely the mission of

**Left: A Whirlwind I of 263 Sqn based at Exeter in 1941. One of only two squadrons to use the Whirlwind, 263 flew many Rhubarb offensive sweeps against the coastal areas of Europe within range, eventually carrying two 227kg (500lb) bombs. The Whirlwind was Britain's pioneer attempt to build a twin-engined fighter with cannon armament. The armament of four 20mm Hispanos was, for its time, devastating; but the Whirlwind was otherwise a poor aircraft because of its unreliable, low-powered engines. A batch of 200 were ordered, but the last 88 were cancelled.**

Above: One of the few photographs of the extremely heavy and specially equipped Lysander IIISCW. This was the type used, from Tempsford and other airfields, to carry agents to enemy territory and, if possible, later bring them back.

Left: After 1940 nearly all Lysanders had their wheel spat covers left off to ease maintenance. This accentuated the utilitarian look of what had become a highly utilitarian STOL aircraft. Most remained in various kinds of operational service, but this example is seen with 54 Operational Training Unit. Light series bomb carriers can be seen attached to the stub wings (intended solely as bomb carriers) attached to the lower ends of the main legs. Pilots frequently flew with the canopy open, when on a warm day the "Lizzie" was one of the most pleasant aircraft in the sky. This example is a Mk III, with poppet-valve Mercury engine; the Perseus-engined machines were even smoother and quieter. Portions of a second aircraft (wheels below fuselage) may just be seen in the background.

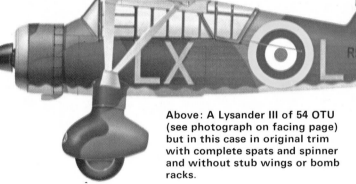

Above: A Lysander III of 54 OTU (see photograph on facing page) but in this case in original trim with complete spats and spinner and without stub wings or bomb racks.

Above: This strikingly striped machine is a target tug Lysander serving in Canada with the RCAF as part of the vast Empire Air Training Plan. One of 325 built at Malton by National Steel Car Corporation, it was in most respects identical to British-built Lysanders apart from having a proportion of North American equipment items. National Steel Car later became Victory Aircraft, building Lancasters and a York, and later Avro Canada and Hawker Siddeley Canada.

the Whirlwind, designed to a specification as early as F.37/35. It was a fine and pleasant machine, and in its slender nose was an unprecedented punch. Yet its development was delayed by engine troubles, the Peregrine being an unhappy outgrowth of the reliable Kestrel; another trouble was that, despite Fowler flaps, the landing speed was 80mph which was incompatible with short grass fields. Eventually only 263 and 137 Sqns used the type, which in combat showed much promise. In August 1941 No 263 escorted Blenheims to Cologne in daylight! Only 112 were built, ending their days as "Whirlibombers" on cross-Channel "Rhubarb" sorties strafing and bombing targets of opportunity.

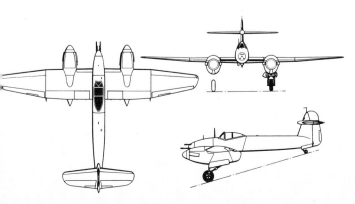

Above: Though instantly identifiable to almost every British schoolboy of the time, the Whirlwind was secret during most of its early career (though featured in Luftwaffe literature).

Left: Three-view of Whirlwind I, without bomb racks.